The
GILROY GARLIC FESTIVAL PLAYBOOK:
For the Love of Garlic and Community

By J. Chris Mickartz & Larry J. Mickartz

PUBLISHED BY:
INFOPOWER COMMUNICATIONS
GILROY, CALIFORNIA

Grateful acknowledgment is hereby given to the following for permission
to reprint from the following sources:

Archived articles and photos acquired from the Gilroy Museum originally published
in The Gilroy Dispatch (Weeklys, A California Local Media Group) from 1978-1994 and the
Gilroy Garlic Festival Special 25th Anniversary edition published in 2004.

Archived photos and marketing materials provided by
the Gilroy Garlic Festival Association.

Photos and copy originally published in gmhTODAY,
The Lifestyles Magazine for South Santa Clara Valley from 2006-2019.

Published by InfoPower Communications
7446 Rosanna Street, Gilroy, CA 95020

Library of Congress Control Number: 2022938096

ISBN Number: 979-8-9861974-0-1

Preface

The Gilroy Garlic Festival has touched so many lives in Gilroy. And, one might say, in most corners of the world. It would be impossible to have lived in Gilroy from 1979 to 2020 without having experienced the Festival on some level, if not directly by being a part of the over 4,000 Gilroyans who helped put it on each year, then by attending or having a family member or friend involved. When asked, "where are you from"—saying "Gilroy" often would be responded to by the reference to the Festival.

The Festival took Gilroy from a small town without much of an identity to being world-renowned as "The Garlic Capital of the World." And although some would argue that the designation might be a bit of a stretch, the pride that it brought to the community, most assuredly, was of world-renowned proportions.

Since its inception, we've been involved in the Festival in one capacity or another. When we started our community magazine, Gilroy TODAY, back in 2006, the Festival became the topic of an entire issue each year. And when we expanded the magazine to cover the South Santa Clara Valley, ghmTODAY featured an area of the Festival each year. Our goal has always been to stroke the flame of pride that the Festival's many volunteers — from Gilroy, Morgan Hill, and San Martin—have had in putting on such a successful event. One can find many of those articles in the pages of this book.

Many sources have provided the photos and background text for this book. Much of the historical information (1978-1994) was obtained from the Gilroy Museum archives of newspaper articles taken from the local paper, The Gilroy Dispatch (Weeklys—A California Media Group). One can find the excerpts under "In The News." Without their assistance and support, this book would not have been possible.

Color photos from 1979-2006 and black and white photos from 1980 and 1982 came from the Gilroy Garlic Festival archives. Over the years, they had a number of photographers taking pictures on their behalf. Although we were unable to identify all of them, a list of those we could identify is located on page 247. We do want to express a special debt of gratitude, however, to Bill Strange, Official Festival photographer from 1982-2016. He captured the essence of the Festival year after year—making it possible for us to share that essence with you.

A special thanks go to members of the community who shared photos, memorabilia, and stories of the Festival: Norie Goforth, Edith Edde, Sam Bozzo, Don Christopher, David Bouchard, Pat DeStasio, Susan Dodd, Barbara Trekell, Brigitte Nichols, Tim Filice, Valerie Filice, just to name a few.

On a final note, we would especially like to acknowledge our copy editors and Festival historians: Susan Valenta, Joann Kessler, and Chris Filice. Thank You!

For a complete list of photographers, contributors and special recognitions, see page 247.

Larry and J. Chris Mickartz

The GILROY GARLIC FESTIVAL PLAYBOOK:
For the Love of Garlic and Community

THE GILROY GARLIC Festival PLAYBOOK

Within These Pages

Contents by the Year

[🧄 In the News] Obtained from the Gilroy Museum archives of newspaper articles taken from the local paper, *The Gilroy Dispatch*

Features

Year One 1979

The Beginning of a Legacy that Would Position Gilroy as the Garlic Capital of the World.

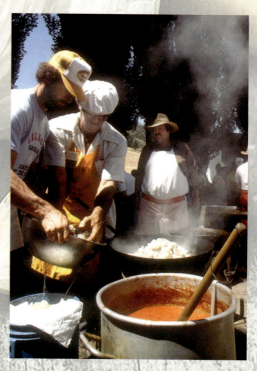

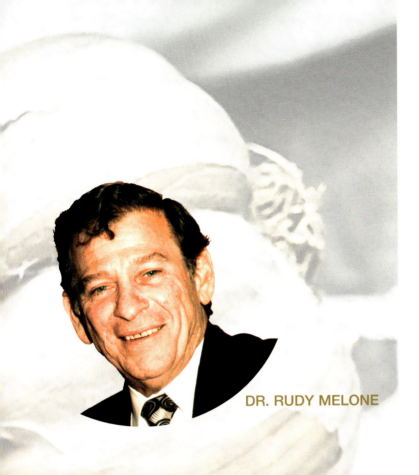

DR. RUDY MELONE

The Festival Story Begins with Dr. Rudy Melone —

In 1978, Rudy had been the President of Gavilan Community College for just a few short years. Once settled in at Gavilan, he felt that he needed to know more about Gilroy in general and its primary industry, farming, specifically. One of the crops that caught his interest was garlic. He felt that one of Gilroy's top products should be a source of pride; not one of embarrassment.

Rudy was also a spokesperson for the Gilroy Chamber of Commerce and often went to the city council to request funds, a task that he thought needed to be remedied. A self-supporting Chamber would eliminate the need to "beg the city for financial support" each year.

It soon became clear to Rudy that a garlic Festival might remedy Gilroy's 'malodorous embarrassments' and raise some money in the process. He became determined to prove that the title "Garlic Capital of the World"—which a small town in France had claimed—rightfully belonged to Gilroy. He envisioned a Festival to celebrate its agricultural product and let people know what an excellent accompaniment a clove of garlic is to so many dishes and prove that Gilroy had the community spirit to make it happen.

The Man

Rudy Melone was a Yankee, born on August 29, 1925, in New Haven, Connecticut. He was of Italian heritage. He was orphaned at two years of age when his mother died giving birth to her second child. According to Gloria, his wife, he rarely spoke of his early years in an orphanage but shared many stories of how he tried to run away to see his father.

When he was about 12, his father took him out of the orphanage and placed him with a foster woman who was an Italian American. That was the first time he felt that he had a family—he had a brother his age and a younger sister—it was a good time. But, it was short-lived when his foster family moved away, and he was placed with a physically abusive woman. Eventually, he went to live with his father, first in New York City and then Portland, Oregon.

He served as a Navy Seabee and was a veteran of World War II. After the war, he used his GI Bill to attend college. He was a consummate scholar with three degrees: BA, MA (Portland, Oregon), and a Ph.D. (Berkeley) in higher education and administration.

His professional career consisted of serving as Dean at Pima College (Tuscan, AZ) and Skyline College (San Mateo, CA) before becoming President of Gavilan Community College from 1975-1985.

After observing the lack of affordable and safe housing for farmworkers and low-income people, Dr. Melone proposed the creation of a non-profit public benefit corporation in 1978. That non-profit was incorporated in 1979 and would be called the South County Housing Corporation and would be responsible for providing housing throughout the region for the next twenty years. He considered it one of his most significant accomplishments.

Dr. Melone was a man who embraced life, was a true humanitarian, and was a great communicator. Although he was a relative newcomer to Gilroy back in 1978, he was a true Gilroyan. He continued to be active in the community even after retiring to San Francisco in 1985.

He died of cancer on September 17, 1998, in San Francisco at 73. He was survived by his wife of 28 years, Gloria, and their three sons—John, Philip, and Michael. He is revered as the father of the Gilroy Garlic Festival, which effectively has altered the history of Gilroy.

Gilroy, the Town that Clove to a Winner

Melone realized Gilroy had been sitting on top of a $50 million industry dead in the center of the region that produces 90% of the world's garlic. Gilroy, weary of the way the Western world tended to wrinkle its nose at a lowly weed like garlic, had virtually been apologizing for that fact.

— Los Angeles Times "View" Orange County 8/7/79

In His Own Words— Rudy Melone

Garlic, How Sweet the Smell!

(Gilroy Dispatch November 6, 1978)

The sunny days of fall filter through our fingers like precious gold coin. How casually we accept them, and spend them. These golden days are laden with healthy sounds, sights, and smells of our area. Truly, South County and San Benito are pretty places—and more.

Indeed, just as carelessly as we indulge ourselves in this special Indian Summer, our senses squander that which confronts our eyes and noses each day. What we are overlooking is those hundreds of acres in our area which produce 90 percent of the fresh garlic consumed in the United States. Ever since 1923, in fact, the fields around Gilroy and San Benito have been the leading garlic producers for our country.

To give you some idea of what that 90 percent means, fresh garlic consumption in the United States is about 128 million pounds per year—just over half a pound per person, and rising each year.

The figures I'm presenting come from the authority of Joseph Gubser and Don Christopher. Gubser has 35 years of experience to inform him, while Christopher is a more recent entrant in the garlic market. They point out that garlic represents a $27 million industry in our area. This is a staggering figure, and gives us some idea of how little we know of our own local agribusiness.

But, fresh garlic has given away in recent times to the dehydrated end of the business. Of that $28 million industry, $20 million is in fresh, while $18 million is in processed garlic—powder, salt, chips, flakes, and so on. The US consumption of these items is 28-30 million pounds per year. Since it takes three pounds of fresh to make one pound of dry, then nearly 94 pounds have to be raised to be processed.

Another interesting aspect of our industry is pointed out by Gubser. Ten to 15 years ago, 80 percent of our market was domestic and 20 percent foreign. Those figures are more near the 50-50 split today. The Gubser and Christopher labels, and a number of others, travel worldwide, as do the brands served by Gilroy Foods, Inc. and Foremost-Gentry.

Much of the $28 million has impact on the local economy, of course. The most significant portion, however, is that which goes into the hands of labor as wages. The fresh industry accounts for a payroll of nearly $2.5 million per year. Gilroy Foods and Gentry processors have payrolls which cannot be disclosed, but with 1,500 to 1,700 employees between them you can imagine the magnitude. Since payroll dollars usually turn over four or five times for the purchase of goods and services, you can get some idea of the impact (no pun intended) of the garlic industry in our area. How sweet, therefore, the smell of garlic!

All the foregoing by the way of pointing out that Thursday, November 9, the Gilroy Rotary Club will honor the garlic industry at its weekly luncheon. Don Christopher will host the mob at his ranch and packaging plant on Bloomfield road. I get to program chairman, and all of us get to feast on a menu of goodies prepared by Val Filice. Imagine yourself seated to a gourmet luncheon of shrimp sautéed in lobster butter and garlic, pasta with a special garlic-based sauce, and fresh vegetables delicately treated with a blended dressing of oil, herbs and garlic. Top it with a lovely white wine and you have a feast worthy of any Rotarian.

Much more space could be consumed telling you more about the value of garlic, the gastronomical goody. Another time for that. I hope this much, however, will give you pause the next time the aroma of garlic fills the air of South County and San Benito, and you realize that it is the sweet smell of success you're breathing in, as well as good health.

"When I sat down over coffee with Rudy, back in 1978, and he explained his ideas for a garlic Festival, I told him he was crazy; nobody was going to respond to garlic that way. But he had it all mapped out and he truly saw the future. He believed that, with the right emphasis and solid community support, this (the garlic Festival) would become a big deal. I laughed at the 20th Anniversary luncheon…when someone asked him if he thought the Garlic Festival would become as big as it has…"
Yeah, he always did."

Val Filice

"There would be no Gilroy Garlic Festival without Rudy. Rudy was a wonderful, tenacious man. The event was his idea and he was the spark that made everything go. He loved Gilroy and because of his Italian heritage, he loved garlic. Putting the two together, he increased the popularity of Gilroy and likewise, garlic. He was a good man and a good friend."

Don Christopher

In His Own Words— Rudy Melone

Garlic Festival One

(Gilroy Dispatch 1979)

It started off small, only last November, as a luncheon program for the Gilroy Rotary Club. The only idea I had in mind was to bring some favorable attention to the oft-ignored multi-million dollar industry of our area—garlic. As Rotarian program chairman for the November meeting, it gave a special flavor (no pun intended) to a month of programs usually heavy with political overtones.

Who would have thought that it would lead to a full-scale garlic Festival? One which might, in fat, become an annual event depending on the success of this first venture on August 4-5, 1979.

Going back, for a moment, it all started with a brief featurette which caught my eye in a Sunday paper. Arleux, it reported, a small town in France, had proclaimed itself the Garlic Capital of the World! Now, how could a community of 2,700 persons make such a statement? But, the article went on, those enterprising French villagers attracted over 70,000 persons to their town during an annual garlic Festival.

Amazing! At least to me. Not that they hadn't the right. What delighted me was the pride they had in their major crop. And the way in which they had given garlic such a positive image. More power to them, I thought, but why not more power to us, too. After all, Gilroy and garlic have been synonymous since early Mexican workers had developed the original garlic cracker.

Garlic, indeed, is part of the Gilroy history. That first garlic cracker became a mechanized process under the astute business mind of Joseph Gubser. Since those early days the Gubser name has been on packages of garlic shipped all over the world. True, too, of Don Christopher, who now raises and distributes more garlic than he does his famous cherries; Gilroy Foods and Gentry dehydrate tons of it into powder, salt, flakes and chips; and, from the ground up and on to consumption around the world garlic now represents a $40-50 million industry in and around Gilroy. Why not be proud of it?!

Suffice to say, the Rotary luncheon was a delightful, gustatory success. Christopher graciously extended the use of his packing plant as the luncheon area. Val Filice, and a friend, cooked up a feast: pasta with garlic sauce, shrimp sautéed in garlic, minestra of garlic dressing, salad, garlic bread and wine from the local vineyards and vintners. More than this, it was the opening event which has led us to the first Gilroy Garlic Festival.

Present at the Rotary luncheon were food editors from newspapers in Los Angeles, San Francisco, and San Jose. The word spread like wildfire about Gilroy and garlic. I received calls from all parts of the country, all asking the same question: "Are you going to do it again and how can I participate?" Well, the time has come and you're all welcome to share in the fun and food.

A great number of people have helped in making Garlic Festival come to life. Following the Rotary success, Christopher; Bert Mantelli, president of the Gilroy Chamber of Commerce; and Jim Oteri and Lynda Trelut of Nob Hill Grocers, contacted me to discuss expanding the luncheon into a full-fledged Festival. The chamber had already approved a sponsorship role, and Nob Hill had been in the vanguard of the "garlic is gorgeous" theme with Pet Garlic, T-shirts, and other promotional idea. In short order the ideas took shape: location options, theme, booths, entertainment, events, and all other forms of trivia were discussed.

The most important topics, however, were: 1) for what purpose(s) is the Festival to be held, and 2) what would be the respective roles of the chamber of commerce and the garlic Festival committee? The answer to number one stayed as my original intention in proposing it to the chamber: the garlic Festival will proudly celebrate the worth of garlic and help create a positive and favorable image of Gilroy; and, secondly, it might derive sufficient revenues to help make the chamber of commerce independent of annual support from the City of Gilroy. The answer to the second item was a bit more complex, and is still in the process of development. Basically, however, it was decided to set up a separate non-profit Garlic Festival Corporation which would be responsible for planning and staging the event utilizing as much assistance from chamber members as possible. After final audit all proceeds would be divided into two parts: a sum would be set aside to assure the necessary base for next year's Festival, and the balance would be turned over to the chamber of commerce operating budget (assuming a balance after only one event).

There's much more to the story, of course, including the many men and women involved in making the event possible.…But, if you want to help, or set up a booth, here are the members of the steering committee you can contact: Rudy Melone, chairman; Don Christopher, vice chairman; Hy Miller, Chamber of Commerce president; Judy Latronica (J. Chris Mickartz), program chairwoman; Bob Dyer, promotions chairman; Bill Ayer, logistics and safety chairman, and Joe Filice, booth sales.

In any event, plan now to join us August 4 and 5—to have fun, and to give cheer in celebration of garlic and Gilroy.

DON CHRISTOPHER

Garlic Was the Driving Force Behind the Development of the Festival

In 1978, Don Christopher started the Fresh Garlic Association to get other garlic shippers together to promote the sale and use of fresh garlic. Little did he know that he and the Association would play an instrumental role in developing a festival that would soon change peoples' perception of garlic for years to come—and give Gilroy the distinction of being the "Garlic Capital of the World."

Don and the Association's role in the first festival's success was immense. Caryl Saunders, a promotions person for the Fresh Garlic Association, invited Betsy Balsley, Food Editor for the Los Angeles Times to the Rotary luncheon on Thursday, November 9th, at Christopher Ranch that ended up being the springboard for the first festival. Betsy suggested the development of a festival and talked Don into participating in the formation of the first Garlic Festival. Don recalls Rudy Melone saying, "Let's do it."

Besides being one of four financial contributors (Gilroy Foods, Nob Hill Foods, Dr. James Cecilian, and Christopher Ranch), Christopher Ranch arranged to use the pasture and house at "Bloomfield Ranch" — where the first festival was to take place. The Ranch donated the use and preparation of the land for a parking lot in addition to furnishing trucks, propane, gas, staff, and, of course, all the garlic.

The Man

Don Christopher was born in San Jose in 1934. His grandfather, Ole, had immigrated to the Santa Clara Valley from Denmark in the 1880's and farmed prunes. As a young boy of 7, Don joined his siblings to work the farm alongside their father, Frank.

Don attended Oak Grove Grammar School, joined the 4H Club and graduated from Live Oak High School, where he was student body president and a forward on the school's championship basketball team.

His business sense seemed to be part of his DNA. By the time Don turned 12, he was setting gopher traps in the field to make a little extra money. As soon as he could drive, he took on a paper route in Capitola.

Being part of a farming family had its interesting moments. Don recalls going with his grandfather, who he remembers looked a bit like a hobo, to a Mercury dealership to help him purchase a car.

"No one wanted to wait on us because we didn't look like we could afford a car."

When a salesman finally asked Don's grandfather just how he expected to pay for a car, he replied very matter-of-factly, "Do you mind cash?"

Fresh out of San Jose State University in 1956, Don came home to Gilroy. He wanted to farm, but felt that prunes were a profitable, yet boringly predictable, business. With a loan from their father, Don and his brother Art purchased 130 acres of farm land and planted lima beans and sugar beets. Don also set aside 10 acres to plant a then not-so-popular crop, garlic.

In addition to following in his grandfather's and father's footsteps in business, Don also followed them in their interest in education and community. Ole Christopher was a trustee at Oak Grove School District back in the days when trustees dug septic tanks for schools. By the time Don's father became a trustee at the same district, the position was a little less hands-on but nonetheless important. Between them they served the district for 25 years and their efforts were acknowledged when one of the district's elementary schools took the Christopher name—another tradition that seems to run in the family.

Don turned 88 years of age in 2022. The hats he has worn throughout his life are many. He is a family-man with a blended family of five children and many grandchildren and even a couple great grandchildren. He is a mentor, a philanthropist, a partner in business with his two sons and the co-founder of the Gilroy Garlic Festival.

His contributions to the community are far reaching. They include financial support to Christopher High School, the Community Arts Center, Gilroy High School, Scholarships throughout the years, CMAP (*Community Media Access Partnership), Gavilan College, the Grange, Christmas Hill Park , the Gilroy Compassion Center and of course, the Gilroy Garlic Festival.

Gilroy Has Truly Got It and It's Just a Great Place to be.

(Excerpts from a Video Interview, Pre2008)

Garlic Capital of the World! Maybe?

Gilroy never really was the Garlic Capital of the World. Of the United States maybe, but the World sounds better, so when it was mentioned in an article, we went with it. We had the biggest shipper, dehydrator, and Festival in California, and maybe the United States. Garlic started in Gilroy before 1900, 1800 something, brought over from Italy and France. We have better quality garlic today than 50 years ago.

Early Memories

Dr. Rudy Melone, principal at Gavilan College and a member of the Gilroy Rotary Club and Gilroy Chamber of Commerce, came up with the idea after reading about the small city in France that held a Festival with an attendance of 70,000 and were the self-proclaimed "Garlic Capital of the World." He went to all his friends, including me, and said, "let's put on a garlic Festival." He got a lot of no's initially, including mine.

He was head of the Rotary Club's program committee, so he pushed to have a small Festival at a Rotary luncheon. I spoke to Caryl Saunders, our Fresh Garlic Association promotions director, and she brought in the various media people, and growers. Just under 300 people attended. A food editor from the Los Angeles Times insisted that Gilroy should have a Festival. "I was sold." Val cooked that day. We started meeting two weeks after that and eight months later, there was a garlic festival.

Side Story

The landlord of the site we had selected for the Festival was to advise the tenant that we would be using the property for the event. They were to move out. It was the perfect spot at the time. We planned for 5000 for two days, food for 3000 people, booths, entertainment, and fun. A regional celebrity, the Green Grocer out of San Francisco, attended.

We had 15,000 people attend. When we sold the tickets, we had to recycle and resell them. We had to go to Monterey, San Jose, and every store in Gilroy for scampi, calamari, and steak. We made money, paid bills, and everyone was happy. The County, however, said we couldn't have it at the same location the following year. So, we moved to Christmas Hill Park.

Initial Reactions

I said, "no, that's impossible. I already have a job, and I don't need another one." Rudy said it would be good for the community, chamber, etc. Once we decided to do it, we needed to figure out who would run the Festival. We first offered it to the Rotary Club President and Mayor of Gilroy, Norman Goodrich. He threw us out of his office. We left very unhappily. Then, we went to the Chamber of Commerce president, Burt Mantelli, and asked if they would like to own it. They said, "NO, we don't want to run it, but we would like the beer concession, and we will help promote the event." So, we decided to go ahead and run it ourselves. We decided to get local labor to help—and then, soon after, decided whoever worked the Festival could pick out their charities, and profits would go to them based on man-hours.

Dynamics of Relationships

The camaraderie created by the Festival was unbelievable. Rudy, the head of the Junior College, and I, a farmer, thought so much alike. And Val was a great chef, and he had the ability to enlist others to help him cook the food.

Rudy Melone

He was a special person, his most admirable quality was that he got along with everybody. You could argue with him without a problem. I recall one year when the Hispanic Labor Union wanted to start a garlic strike before the Festival. Instead of making a big deal out of it, he invited them to spend the night at Gavilan College and picket the next day. He was such a people person, and he had an elaborate vocabulary and way of doing things that were just amazing.

Val Filice

I met Val five years before the Festival. He grew prunes and garlic also, so I got to know him well. He was just bigger than life—real special person. He cooked at Christopher Ranch for our Christmas party three years before. All the items he cooked for the Festival luncheon were the same as he served at the party. I remember going to various media TV stations, and he would cook the calamari flame-up in front of the cameras. One year he almost burned down the building—it ended up being the best promotion we had. Everyone wanted to come and see the flames. Val was responsible for it all.

He was a great ally as well. I remember when I wanted to expand the Festival to three days and the board at the time voted it down. I knew I was right, so I enlisted Val—we went to the board asking that they extend the Festival to three days or two weekends but felt three days would be much better than two weekends.

The Community

The people in Gilroy are so amazing; many people from around the area have helped with the Festival. Each year, more and more people wanted to work at the Festival. I am so proud that the monies raised have gone to non-profits over the years. Of course, some funds were set aside for purchases in the community—parks, etc. Before the Festival, Gilroy was just another small town, nothing anyone would write home about. "Kilroy," freeway, not very popular or even noticed. After the Festival, lots of media attention changed the complexion of the community.

The Pre-Festival Activities...

THE QUEEN PAGEANT

The First Annual "Miss Garlic Festival" Beauty Pageant was held on July 31, 1979 at the Gilroy High School Theatre. The Pageant Chairman was Regina Read and her committee consisted of Roberta Anderson and Shirley Currie (all three had held the title of "Miss Gilroy") with Rudy Melone. The Master of Ceremonies for the first pageant was Bob Taylor.

GREAT GARLIC Cook-Off

The first Recipe Contest/Cook-Off was held the morning of the Festival at Gavilan College. Norie Goforth (l) and Rose Emma Pelliccione (r) crowned the first winner Kelly Greene of Mill Valley. There were 500 plus entries.

PET GARLIC

Nob Hill Stores caged garlic for pet owners and emblazoning local fame on T-shirts. Melissa Oteri, whose picture is on the side of the carton containing "Pet Garlic," displays its contents as she wears a shirt inscribed "Gilroy Garlic Capital of the World." The Pet Garlic was the brainchild of Joe Oteri and Lynda Trelut of Nob Hill Stores.

MISS GARLIC FESTIVAL

Kathleen (Katie) Bendel became the first Miss Garlic Festival. At the time she was 17 and had lived in Gilroy for 12 years with her parents Roland and Barbara Bendel. She was a 1979 graduate of Gilroy High School and had plans to attend Gavilan College. She was crowned by Rose Emma Pelliccione, Miss Garlic 1955. Trophies were presented by Mayor Norman Goodrich.

BARN DANCE

Held on July 14th to raise funds for the first Garlic Festival. Approximately 500 people attended.

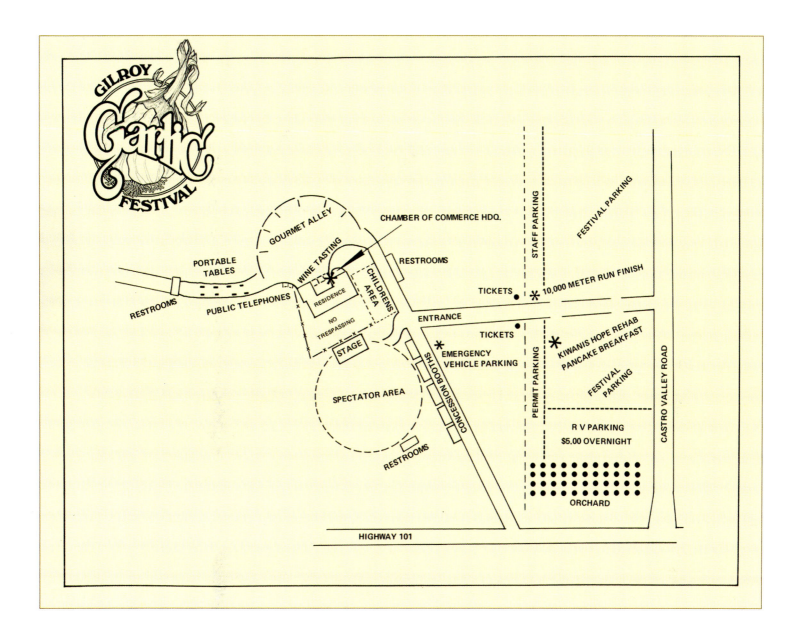

The Place...

A few days before August 4, 1979, a group of volunteers showed up at the Bloomfield Ranch (located west of the on-ramp to Highway 25 from 101 South) to set up for the first Garlic Festival. Mort McCloud owned the mansion on the property but it was leased out to a family. As the story goes, Mr. McCloud forgot to advise his tenants that there was going to be a festival at their residence. So, when the crews showed up to prepare the grounds, they were greeted by two very large dogs and a very confused tenant. By the time Rudy Melone was done talking to them, the festival organizers were given access to not only the grounds but the house and office.

The first Garlic Festival was the only festival that was not at Christmas Hill Park.

The Event...

The first Garlic Festival in 1979 was held on August 3-4 and was the only Festival that was not at Christmas Hill Park. The first location was Bloomfield Ranch, west of the on-ramp to Highway 25 from 101 South.

Food items in Gourmet Alley were calamari, scampi, pasta con pesto, broiled garlic mushrooms, garlic pepper steak sandwich, and garlic bread. The Jaycees took care of parking, and a variety of community groups manned booths to sell food and garlic-related items.

One of the event highlights was a tethered hot air balloon ride. Erratic winds, however, cut the rides short. On the grounds, there was entertainment and a children's area on site. And offsite, at Gilroy High School, there was a "big event" on Saturday night—a concert featuring Larry Hosford, a popular bluegrass/country group, and Johnny Rusk, an Elvis impersonator. In addition, the Kiwanis Club hosted a breakfast.

The Great Garlic Gallop (10,000-meter race) finished at the back of the grounds so the runners could go directly into the Festival. The first recipe contest was held at Gavilan College, with the winners introduced on the Festival stage. The winning recipes were passed out at the Festival grounds.

Those who worked or attended the first Festival remember the extraordinary energy. The organizers expected, at the most, 5,000 visitors, but 15,000 showed up! Parking was an issue. And running out of many food items in Gourmet Alley precipitated trips to supermarkets in Gilroy, Morgan Hill, and Hollister to purchase all the butter, shrimp, calamari, and bread they could find. There was not enough water, restrooms, or space in general, but people had fun.

That first Festival represented a rough start for an event that would be known worldwide and put Gilroy on the map. The initial contribution of $15,000 to the community has grown to a cumulative total of over $12 million. The sense of community and identity visitors have seen over the past 40-plus years results from that excellent town party held so long ago.

From Day One

The thought was to avoid the stagnation in past Festivals that seemingly fizzled out because of loss of enthusiasm. The goal was to have a continuous flow of new people and new ideas, which would keep the Festival fresh and exciting. It was always about renewal through the constant infusion of new people and new ideas. The concept was to have chairs serve two years, with an assistant chair which would then become chair for two years—constantly training and bringing new people into the mix. Past chairs had the opportunity to move into the advisory board, board of directors, and officer positions.

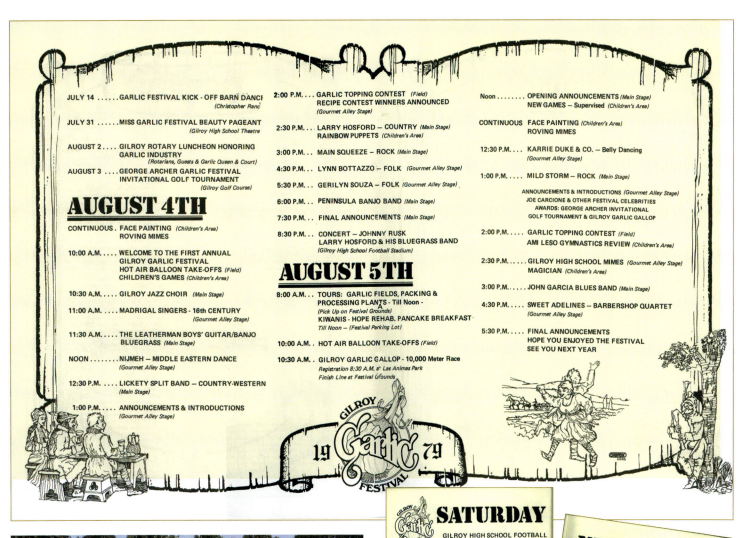

JULY 14 ...... GARLIC FESTIVAL KICK - OFF BARN DANCE
(Christopher Ranch)

JULY 31 ...... MISS GARLIC FESTIVAL BEAUTY PAGEANT
(Gilroy High School Theatre)

AUGUST 2 .... GILROY ROTARY LUNCHEON HONORING
GARLIC INDUSTRY
(Rotarians, Guests & Garlic Queen & Court)

AUGUST 3 .... GEORGE ARCHER GARLIC FESTIVAL
INVITATIONAL GOLF TOURNAMENT
(Gilroy Golf Course)

AUGUST 4TH

CONTINUOUS . FACE PAINTING (Children's Area)
ROVING MIMES

10:00 A.M. .... WELCOME TO THE FIRST ANNUAL
GILROY GARLIC FESTIVAL
HOT AIR BALLOON TAKE-OFFS (Field)
CHILDREN'S GAMES (Children's Area)

10:30 A.M. .... GILROY JAZZ CHOIR (Main Stage)

11:00 A.M. .... MADRIGAL SINGERS - 16th CENTURY
(Gourmet Alley Stage)

11:30 A.M. .... THE LEATHERMAN BOYS' GUITAR/BANJO
BLUEGRASS (Main Stage)

NOON .... NIJMEH — MIDDLE EASTERN DANCE
(Gourmet Alley Stage)

12:30 P.M. .... LICKETY SPLIT BAND — COUNTRY-WESTERN
(Main Stage)

1:00 P.M. .... ANNOUNCEMENTS & INTRODUCTIONS
(Gourmet Alley Stage)

2:00 P.M. .... GARLIC TOPPING CONTEST (Field)
RECIPE CONTEST WINNERS ANNOUNCED
(Gourmet Alley Stage)

2:30 P.M. ... LARRY HOSFORD — COUNTRY (Main Stage)
RAINBOW PUPPETS (Children's Area)

3:00 P.M. ... MAIN SQUEEZE — ROCK (Main Stage)

4:30 P.M. ... LYNN BOTTAZZO — FOLK (Gourmet Alley Stage)

5:30 P.M. ... GERILYN SOUZA — FOLK (Gourmet Alley Stage)

6:00 P.M. ... PENINSULA BANJO BAND (Main Stage)

7:30 P.M. ... FINAL ANNOUNCEMENTS (Main Stage)

8:30 P.M. ... CONCERT — JOHNNY RUSK
LARRY HOSFORD & HIS BLUEGRASS BAND
(Gilroy High School Football Stadium)

AUGUST 5TH

8:00 A.M. ... TOURS: GARLIC FIELDS, PACKING &
PROCESSING PLANTS - Till Noon -
(Pick Up on Festival Grounds)
KIWANIS - HOPE REHAB. PANCAKE BREAKFAST
Till Noon — (Festival Parking Lot)

10:00 A.M. . HOT AIR BALLOON TAKE-OFFS (Field)

10:30 A.M. . GILROY GARLIC GALLOP - 10,000 Meter Race
Registration 8:30 A.M. at Las Animas Park
Finish Line at Festival Grounds

Noon .... OPENING ANNOUNCEMENTS (Main Stage)
NEW GAMES — Supervised (Children's Area)

CONTINUOUS FACE PAINTING (Children's Area)
ROVING MIMES

12:30 P.M. ... KARRIE DUKE & CO. — Belly Dancing
(Gourmet Alley Stage)

1:00 P.M. ... MILD STORM — ROCK (Main Stage)

ANNOUNCEMENTS & INTRODUCTIONS (Gourmet Alley Stage)
JOE CARCIONE & OTHER FESTIVAL CELEBRITIES
AWARDS: GEORGE ARCHER INVITATIONAL
GOLF TOURNAMENT & GILROY GARLIC GALLOP

2:00 P.M. ... GARLIC TOPPING CONTEST (Field)
AMI LESO GYMNASTICS REVIEW (Children's Area)

2:30 P.M. ..... GILROY HIGH SCHOOL MIMES (Gourmet Alley Stage)
MAGICIAN (Children's Area)

3:00 P.M. .... JOHN GARCIA BLUES BAND (Main Stage)

4:30 P.M. .... SWEET ADELINES — BARBERSHOP QUARTET
(Gourmet Alley Stage)

5:30 P.M. .... FINAL ANNOUNCEMENTS
HOPE YOU ENJOYED THE FESTIVAL
SEE YOU NEXT YEAR

GILROY Garlic FESTIVAL 1979

MAIN STAGE FEATURED A NUMBER OF BANDS

SECOND STAGE FEATURED SMALL ACTS AND ANNOUNCEMENTS

GARLIC TOPPING CONTEST WAS HELD ON FESTIVAL GROUNDS

GOURMET ALLEY

BALLOON RIDE

GROUNDS AND VENDORS

GILROY GARLIC GALLOP

Offsite Tidbits

Gilroy Rotary Club saluted the garlic industry at their Thursday, August 2, 1979 luncheon.

Gilroy Chamber of Commerce sponsored a garlic BBQ on Friday, August 3, to kick off the George Archer golf tournament at the Gilroy Golf Course.

Kiwanis put on a Pancake Breakfast to benefit the HOPE Project on Sunday, August 5, at the Festival grounds parking lot.

Joe Carcione, the Green Grocer, appeared on the Festival grounds on Sunday, August 5, to meet the public and sign autographs. He had a daily syndicated show, viewed in major cities throughout the U.S. He boasted that many of his recipes were strongly laced with garlic.

A&D Christopher Ranch provided garlic industry tours a their packing plant and fields and **Gilroy Foods** had tours of their facilities also on Sunday. Buses took festival-goers to each of the tour locations.

Gilroy Garlic Gallop 10,000-meter run was held on Sunday, July 5. Registration was at Las Animas Park. Some 543 runners ran 6.2 miles. Gilbert Munoz finished 32:14. Paula Jackson was the first woman across the finish line.

Mr. Garlic... Blame It on the Pumpkin!

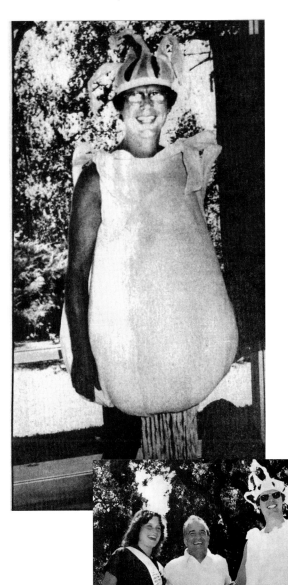

Mr. Garlic with Katy Bendel, 1979 Festival Queen and Joe Carcione, the Green Grocer.

The "Mr. Garlic" story began in 1978 when Bob Kraemer dressed up as a pumpkin for a Halloween party. As the plan progressed for the first Garlic Festival, Ken Vantress, Bob Kraemer's boss at Gilroy Foods, remembered the pumpkin costume. He asked Bob if he— actually his wife, Joanne— could make a similar garlic costume and would he wear it to the legendary Rotary Garlic Luncheon at Christopher Ranch. And so "Mr. Garlic" made his first appearance, and Bob Kraemer would wander the grounds of the first Garlic Festival as "Mr. Garlic."

Sweet Smell of Success
Garlic Festival 1979 by the Numbers

Dr. Rudy Melone presented a check for $1,000 to Hy Miller, president of the Gilroy Chamber of Commerce, acknowledging one of the Festival's two primary goals—to assist the Chamber in its quest to become self-sufficient. The second goal was to promote Gilroy and its major industry, garlic.

Gross Income: $66,090

Net Income: $23,905

Expenses: $42,185

Five "Gourmet Alley" chefs and two support groups designated five non-profit groups to benefit from their efforts: Muscular Dystrophy Association, Gilroy Elks Lodge, Live Oak High School Regime Band Boosters, Hope Rehabilitation Center and Gilroy High School Student Body Fund.

Retained for future: $18,355
Other booths at the Garlic Festival earned an estimated $40,000

— **Gilroy Dispatch 11/21/79**

Gourmet Alley
Val Filice will not share his calamari recipe that was served with a hefty hunk of crusty French bread but all 500 plus entries in the Great Garlic Cook-off will be printed in a cookbook and published by the Festival committee.

Amount of Food

530 lbs	Calamari
250 lbs	Shrimp (Scampi)
700 lbs	Top Sirloin
250 lbs	Green Peppers
450 lbs	Pasta
15 gal	Olive Oil
750	Loaves of French Bread
200 lbs	Fresh Mushrooms
300 lbs	Garlic

Norman Stumpf of Sacramento said he had been to a lot of food events and "The Garlic Festival was truly unique — everything was first class." He confessed that he had "sampled everything."

— **San Jose Mercury News / Mary Phillips 8/8/79**

Fast Facts:
15,000 people attended the first Festival.
Booth fees were $200.
The weather was mild; just missing an earlier heat wave.
Approximately 1,000 volunteers helped put on the Festival.

Kelly's Asian Chicken

Kelly Green of Mill Valley was the first place winner of the first Gilroy Garlic Festival Cook-Off that was held on the morning of the Festival at Gavilan College.

Ingredients

3-3½ Lbs		Frying chicken (cut into serving pieces)
1-3	Tbsp	Peanut Oil
¼	Cup	Soy Sauce
½	Cup	White Vinegar (distilled)
3	Tbsp	Honey
1	Head	Garlic (not cloves) (peeled and coarsley chopped)
1-2	Small	Dried Hot Red Peppers (optional)

Heat oil in large heavy skillet and brown chicken well on all sides, add garlic and peppers toward end. Add remaining ingredients and cook over medium high heat until chicken is done and sauce has been reduced somewhat. This will not take long (less than 10 minutes if pieces are small) and if you have white meat mixed with dark, it should be removed earlier so it doesn't dry out. One must watch the dish carefully to see that the sauce does not burn or boil away. There should be a quantity of sauce left to serve with the chicken and the chicken should appear slightly glazed. Serve with rice or Chinese noodles.

Special thanks to Cathy Katavich for preparing this dish and providing a photograph of it.

Tim Filice sautéed calamari.

KPIX's Evening Magazine Shoots Film in Gilroy… Garlic Festival Featured on TV

Val Filice tasted his famous pasta sauce.

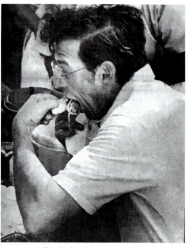

Rudy Melone gave his approval.

LIGHTS, CAMERA, ACTION — San Francisco-based television station KPIX sent their crews to experience the Festival cuisine. It was featured on "Evening Magzine" with then-anchor Steve Fox and company. Gourmet Alley chairperson Tim Filice and Val Filice and the Gourmet Alley master chefs created some soon-to-be Alley staples for the crew, who left with some great footage and full stomachs.

Media Headlines & Quotes

GILROY ISSUES GARLICKY CHALLENGE. *We are confident that the spirit of Gilroy Garlic Festival will linger on. Gilroy gives gargantuan gastronomic gathering for garlic.*
— **San Jose Mercury News 8/1/79**

You could call the town of Gilroy fragrant and friendly. As the local crops are harvested you can follow your nose to Garlic City, USA. The festival was one of those happy bits of Americana when the whole town turns out.
— **Marjorie Rice, Copy News Service 8/79**

GILROY'S BREATHTAKING CELEBRATION. *Garlic-laced specialties were prepared in gigantic pans from morning to night as wave after wave of festival goers followed their noses to the bustling outdoor kitchen area.*
— **Reporter, Vacaville 8/12/79**

The sweet, garlicky smell of success in Gilroy. By any measure, it was a success. — **San Francisco Examiner 8/8/79**

The ultimate in summer food fairs.
— **Los Angeles Herald Examiner 8/7/79**

Garlic town savors the smell of success.
— **New York Times 8/6/80**

THE GREAT GARLIC FESTIVAL—*It was rollicking good fun and the food was super .... God isn't it wonderful to be able to just dive into food because it smells and looks so good and not have to admire it as a work of art first.*
—**San Francisco Chronicle 8/6/80**

Garlic may be a lot of things but now it's cause for celebration — **Chicago Tribune 8/25/79**

Garlic's time has come. Fame's nothing to sniff at in Gilroy. Garlic breathes new life into a town.
— **The Washington Post 8/7 /79**

Garlic was the star of the show. — **Honolulu Advertiser 8/15/79**

Gilroy, California, which claims the title of Garlic Capital of the World, held its first Garlic Festival last week ... there's something about garlic that creates excitement. People can get real loose around garlic.
— **Time Magazine 8/20/79**

GARLIC CAPITAL OF THE WORLD
Gilroy—the town that clove to a winner.
— **Los Angeles Times 8/7/79**

GARLIC IS GOLD FOR GILROY. *Community leaders agreed that the time had come for garlic to come storming out of the pantry closet.*
— **Sacramento Bee 8/12/79**

You could wash down the garlic sauce on garlic bread with garlic wine.
— **London Daily Mail 8/11/79**

Memories

By Valerie Filice

Joe Sillano making "Bagno" Garlic Bread

Garlic Bread

This is my grandfather, Joe Sillano (above photo). He and my grandmother, Florence, were in charge of the all the garlic bread for the first several festivals. He is stirring the "bagno" that the garlic bread was dipped in. Bagno in Italian means bath. My brother, Bob and I grew up calling it "bagna".

All the loaves of bread had to be cut by hand until my grandfather decided to bring his band saw. He and my grandmother stood all day long cutting the bread with the band saw. This certainly sped-up the process—until someone deemed it too dangerous.

Prepping Garlic

I remember my mom (Elsie Filice) being in our home kitchen using her Cuisinart to chop all the garlic used in what today is called Gourmet Alley. She used it so long that she burned up the motor and my dad (Val Filice) had to buy her a new one. She also informed my dad that she was not doing that again. LOL

The Flame Up

The calamari flame up came to fruition by accident. My dad was out at Christopher Ranch to do a demonstration for the media. A small burner was placed on a stage. My dad was then ready to show how calamari was cooked.

My dad had the huge frying pan ready with the olive oil warming, but the media wasn't quite ready. So the oil kept getting hotter and hotter. When the press was finally ready, my dad threw in the calamari, and flames shot up about 3 feet—surprising my dad. The media thought that was normal and loved it, and that's how the famous flame-up started. All by accident.

The famous Garlic Festival flame-ups have as many stories as there have

Val and Elsie making a pot of pasta in the early days.

been festivals. But one of the best stories involves our first Festival at Christmas Hill Park. The "Alley" was set up in the BBQ area, surrounded by lovely shade trees. At that time, the Gilroy Parks and Recreation was run by Bill Ayer. Bill informed my dad that he better not hurt the trees with the flame-ups. Well, of course, that didn't happen, and one of the trees got scorched severely. Being the farmer my dad was, he just pruned the injured branches off the tree. That wasn't good enough for Bill Ayer, so my brother and dad ended up having to replace that tree.

1980

Year Two

Queen Jennette Arde

Christopher Ranch booth at the 1980 Festival… the location, on the way to the Amphitheater stage, remained the same for every Festival to follow.

Al Hansen from Gilroy Foods donned the costume and served as the garlic good-will ambassador until 1988. Patti Stephens was known as "Mrs. Garlic" for all her work managing "Mr. Garlic."

> **The first board of directors served for both the 1979 and the 1980 Festivals. They consisted of Dr. Rudy Melone (president), Don Christopher (vice-president), Lynda Trelut (secretary), Joe Filice (treasurer), Hy Miller (director) and Dave Sorenson (director).**

Attendance quadrupled to 60,000 in the Festival's second year, starting a trend of great popularity. With the significant jump in numbers from the first to second year, Founder Rudy Melone's dream of having a successful event to celebrate garlic came true. "It couldn't have gone better," he noted.

The first chairperson for Gourmet Alley, Tim Filice, remembered how uncertain the association was about who would attend the Festival. "Back then, we were experiencing so much growth; we could never really estimate how many people would show up," he said. "In the early years, we faced different challenges than they do now. It was a lot of fun anticipating how many people would come."

"I've enjoyed every minute of it," said Mike Nowakowski, a cook in Gourmet Alley, where garlic laden scampi and calamari kept all the cooks busy.

Moving the Festival to Christmas Hill Park gave the association more room to work and an excellent amphitheater for entertainment. And the dust-covered parking lot filled-up like Candlestick Park's lot when a baseball game was taking place.

In general, the Festival was well organized and entertaining. And Festival-goers and the organizers were pleasantly surprised that the event would run so smoothly.

One attendee, an architect from Petaluma, Chuck Hildreth, remarked, "I never realized there were so many people who enjoyed having bad breath."

Norie Goforth, the chairperson of the Barn Dance, held a couple of weeks before the Festival, remembers everyone having a good time: "There was no rowdiness and no problems." The barn at Christopher Ranch, home to the pounds of garlic that were to produce the wonderful garlicky foods at Gourmet Alley, was filled with people wall to wall. 🧄

AUGUST 2nd and 3rd, 1980
FESTIVAL OPENS AT 10 AM, CLOSES AT 7 PM
GOURMET FOOD ● ENTERTAINMENT

INTERESTING TIDBIT —

Bill Ayer Eats His Hat

In the Garlic Festival's second year, Bill Ayer kept a promise – sort of – to eat his hat. While helping to organize the first Festival that took place in 1979, he said he didn't think attendance would surpass 5,000. Much to everyone's surprise, it went over 15,000 guests. "I said I'll eat my hat if we get more than 5,000," he said. "So they made me a chocolate cake 'hat' which I had to eat. It was a pleasure."

Attendance
60,000

What Was New
Event Moved to Christmas Hill Park
Arts & Crafts Alley Established
Media Coverage Extensive
Barn Dance Doubled in Attendance
Open Tennis Tournament

Queen Jennette Arde

1980
Garlic Festival
Archive Photos

[🧄 In the News]

Parking and Safety Concerns Arise

Representing the Festival (photo above) were Dave Sorenson, Allen Greco, Bill Ayer, Darrel Shuck, Harry Hammelev and John Garcia.

Months of planning went into securing Christmas Hill Park as the site for the Festival and into channeling traffic to and from without causing problems for the city.

To solve the problem, Darrel Shuck made 85 signs to guide traffic from the off-ramp north to Thomas Road, where it would head west and south to Santa Teresa Boulevard and then onto Miller Avenue to a large field north of the eucalyptus trees. Cars leaving the lot on Miller Avenue would return to Santa Teresa and may then head north or south as desired to leave the area. Beyond the lot, Miller Avenue traffic was one-way only, from north to south.

Media Coverage Overwhelming

The Garlic Festival's traveling television show, starring the 1980 Festival Queen, Jennette Arde, spokesperson Karen Christopher and chef Val Filice, spent many hours and covered many miles in the weeks before the second Festival.

For their efforts, the Festival received coverage on a number of TV stations from throughout California. And many major newspapers sent writers and photographers to the Festival.

"Last year, the novelty of the tag "Garlic Capital of the World" drew TV crews and nationwide newspaper reporters; this year, the flood of press was not depleted one bit," noted Christopher. She added that trying to drum up publicity for the first Festival was like pulling teeth, but world title was the international pitch that made the difference.

Returning from a taping of "The Dinah Shore" show following the 1979 Festival were, from left to right: Karen Christopher, Mayor Norm Goodrich, Val and Elsie Filice, Don Christopher and Katy Bendel.

Gilroy's Carol Bannister showed some of the same style that worked well for Ginger Rogers in her dance routine with Fred Astaire at the Garlic Festival Golf Tournament.

After some lively dancing, it's nice to rest on a hay bale, especially when you get a kiss from a friend. Pictured at the 1980 Garlic Festival Barn Dance are Julie Palia and Scott Donnelly.

Gourmet Alley…
Not an Ordinary Food Booth

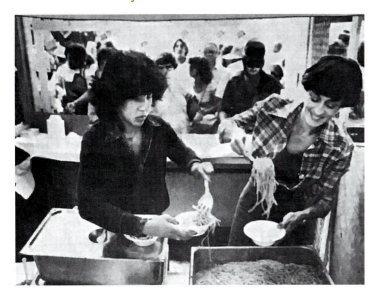

"The logistics are mind-boggling," noted Tim Filice, Gourmet Alley Chairman. "Blueprints? Flow charts? You Bet!"

"It's much more complicated than putting on one booth. For one thing, the crowd estimates for the two days swing widely from double the first year's attendance of 20,000 to an overwhelming 80,000. We're buying food by the ton — literally. It's squirreled all over town and held in reserve," Filice advised just before the opening day.

As in the first year, Filice tapped into local chefs, asking them to donate their time, businesses to donate money, and suppliers to donate food.

Val Filice, the head chef, was tasked with overseeing the cooking of the calamari, scampi, garlic bread, and a new item — stir fry fresh local vegetables with garlic. Jim Rubino was in charge of stuffed mushrooms and a new offering of salad with a garlic dressing; Fred Domino, ingredients and Paul Filice, equipment.

"Another reason for the popularity of Gourmet Alley, besides the fact that the food was so good, was the outdoor kitchen, a lot of animation, and people enjoyed watching the flame shoot up," noted Filice.

Area Designated for Arts & Crafts

In response to evaluations expressing unhappiness about the mixed exhibits at the first Festival, where arts and crafts booths were blended in with food and commercial booths, it was decided that there should be an Arts & Crafts Alley.

About 30 booths, including ceramics, painting, hand-made sunbonnets, stained glass, plant holders, and other items, lined the pathway on the eastern part of the park, beyond the amphitheater but close to the new entrance to the park that was built specifically for the Festival.

Then, chairman Kent Child stated, "We feel that the Arts and Crafts Alley will provide an enjoyable sideshow to the Festival, where people may browse or visit if they get bored with music at the two entertainment centers."

City's Economy Gets a Boost

The Festival's impact was felt far beyond the confines of the award-winning Christmas Hill Park, where this year's Festival events are concentrated. Local motel operators will not display any vacancy signs during the weekend as most available rooms were reserved weeks ago.

Although gas stations certainly are expected to do a land-office business, how much merchants will immediately accrue (additional revenue) is unknown. And retailers are hoping that many Festival-goers will return to Gilroy another time to browse local shops.

The garlic industry already is big business in Gilroy, with two of the nation's largest garlic processing plants—Gilroy Foods, a subsidiary of McCormick & Co. of Maryland, and Foremost-Gentry—located on Pacheco Pass Highway. Also, fresh garlic packers and growers, including Joseph Gubser and Don Christopher, are among the biggest in the business.

City administrator Fred Wood expects Festival-goers to spend between $200,000 to $300,000. And the city will receive a share of the proceeds through sales tax generation.

Most of the ingredients going into the mouthwatering garlicky foods to be sold and prepared on Gourmet Alley are purchased from locally.

Melone said the community might not notice some effects of the Festival for years.

"There will be a lot of business and industrial people coming to the Festival. They'll see Gilroy differently, which can't help but enhance Gilroy and the whole South County," he said.

In Mayor Norman Goodrich's opinion, the Garlic Festival has caught on better than any community-wide event in the city's past, including the immensely popular gymkhana—the large parade held in Gilroy for more than 30 years until the mid-1950s.

The Garlic Festival could spell financial self-sufficiency for the Chamber of Commerce, thus ending an annual trek to city hall to petition the council for funds. In fact, the Chamber is banking on the Festival to generate a substantial portion of this year's budget.

The Chamber's budget shows $16,000 coming from Festival proceeds. Last year, the Chamber realized approximately $7,500 from beer sales, and the organization again this year has the lucrative concession.

The balance sheet for last year's Festival shows a gross income of $66,090 derived from ticket sales, Gourmet Alley proceeds, the barn dance, booth rentals, program sales, and advertising.

Of the $23,905 net income, $1,000 went to the Chamber, and $4,500 was divided among five Gourmet Alley chefs and two support groups, who designated that profits go to five local non-profit groups. In addition, many non-profit groups earned money through Festival participation.

The Board of Directors

Tim Filice
Vice-President

Norie Goforth
Secretary

Bill Ayer
President

Allen Greco
Treasurer

Jon Voorhies
Director

In 1981, the third year of the Festival, **Bill Ayer**, the Gilroy Parks & Recreation Department Director, served as president. When interviewed in 2003, he noted that he had volunteered at the event every year since the beginning days and served in several capacities.

Ayer served as the logistics chairman of the first two Festivals. He remembers organizing the facilities as a learning experience that paved the way for Festival success.

"Logistics was everything," he said. "It was parking, water, power, restrooms, security, loading all the stuff and getting it there. It was a comedy of errors that first year. It was trying to put together all the ingredients of the Festival. We really didn't know what would happen until we got all the ingredients together."

Moving the Festival to Christmas Hill Park in its second year caused some controversy. Some thought it improper to take the use of the park from residents for the multiple days needed for set-up, tear-down, and the event.

"I was trying to get the parks to be the centerpiece of Gilroy's life at the time," he said. "I thought it was a good idea to bring the Festival there."

"At that time, we didn't have the Ranch Site," Ayer recalls. "Everything was contained at Christmas Hill Park's original site. It was a jam. I remember running out of everything from restrooms to peppers for pepper steak sandwiches."

"Gilroy is a nice little community to live in," he said. "When you live here for a while, you get to know there's a lot of community pride and connectedness. And one of the things that helped create that community pride is the Festival."

The third year of the Festival attracted about 90,000 people, four times the number in the first year.

Some credit was given to an article titled "Take a deep breath and read all about the big garlic trend centered around the Gilroy Garlic Festival," published in the Wall Street Journal (circulation of two million). Don Christopher attributed at least a five thousand increase in attendance to that one article.

"Now, any place I go in the world, I tell them I'm from Gilroy, and they say, 'Oh, the Garlic Capital,'" Ayer said. "It turned Gilroy around—gave it identification. Once the Garlic Festival happened, the townspeople started to gain some pride in themselves and pride in the city."

Ayer retired from the Parks and Recreation Department in 1987. ◄

Attendance

90,000

What Was New

Dave Bouchard was hired as the first paid Office Manager of the Gilroy Garlic Festival Association

Annual barn dance officially named Garlic Squeeze Barn Dance

First Parking Committee Formed

Queen Julie Dunlap

INTERESTING TIDBIT —

Birth of Garlic Flavored Ice Cream

Gentry, which was owned by Foremost McKesson, wanted to showcase the company's various products — namely garlic and dairy — ergo garlic ice cream. The trick was to have the ice cream look like a garlic bulb perched on an ice cream cone. Volunteers would bark "GET your FREE Garlic Ice Cream here!"

Queen Julie Dunlap

THE GILROY GARLIC FESTIVAL PLAYBOOK

[In the News]

Danny Kaye Visits Festival

Garlic had always had a special place at Danny Kaye's table, so his visit to the 1981 Festival proved an amazing time for him and the Festival. He said of his visit and meeting with Val Filice, "He just stood there with his arms out and said, 'What do you think of this and little Gilroy?' That's when I fell in love with the whole thing." Kaye returned the next day with some friends. When asked why, he said he loved the whole idea and was impressed by the friendly attitude of the people, "their enthusiasm about garlic, and the Festival." He also noted that he wanted to try all the food.

The Melone's Take First Place in Cook-Off

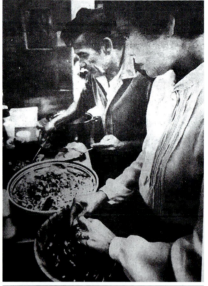

Always the Founder, never a Cook-Off competitor, Rudy Melone fulfilled his second wish this year when he and his wife, Gloria, worked together and presented their Fettucine Gloriosa to a judging panel. The panel consisted of food editors from Bon Appetit magazine, the Boston Globe, Christian Science Monitor, the Sacramento Bee, The Dispatch, and Vern Langerasse, host of a syndicated television show "The Hollywood Chef."

Although questioned in jest about his prestige—having been the inspiration for the Festival— it was clear that Rudy did not influence the panel of five that judged the contest. He and Gloria had a winning recipe that they prepared to perfection.

"Every year, we wanted to enter, and of course, we couldn't," he said. In the meantime, his eyesight failed. Cooking goes better now when he and his wife work together. Their creations are indeed a testament to their "true partnership."

Barn Dance Gets New Name

Norie Goforth and Don Christopher toss garlic at the Christopher Ranch barn, where Garlic Festival Barn Dance will occur. The newly renamed event — Garlic Squeeze Barn Dance— also announced that it would be open only to those over the age of 21. The garlic popcorn was free, but the hot dogs and drinks were an additional charge. The event took place on July 25th, just one week before the Festival.

First Annual Garlic Criterium

Bicycle racers from all over Northern California participated in the first annual Garlic Criterium that took place in downtown Gilroy Sunday, August 2. In four of the five multi-lap events, racers were licensed amateur competitors with the United States Cycling Federation (USCF). But a five-lap stock handicap race was held for 10-speed riders who wanted to try their luck and skill.

Early Staff

First Executive Director, David Bouchard 1981-1986

Loyce Lombard
Administrative Assistant
1981-1994

(See Story, page 95)

David Bouchard was hired in 1981 as the first Director of the Gilroy Garlic Festival Association. He served in that position for six years, ending his tenure in 1986 to become the Executive Director of the Gilroy Chamber of Commerce. He served in that position for the following 13 years.

Originally the Garlic Festival shared an office with the Gilroy Chamber of Commerce on the corner of Monterey and IOOF Streets. However, within one year, the Association, needing more room, looked for their own space. Their new office was located in the Old Gilroy Hotel (now the home of Neon Exchange) on Monterey Street. David recalls his fellow office dwellers fondly: KFAT Radio and the then up-and-coming Los Banos native, Rusty Areias, who would become a State Assemblyman.

The Association resided there for a couple of years before relocating to a larger space (on the northern corner of First and Westwood Drive) that would accommodate the growing Association. That location would be the Association's home for the remainder of David's time served as Director.

Julie Miller was the first administrative assistant for the Association. David would then hire Loyce Lombard for that position. David and Loyce were the only two paid employees of the Festival. Edith Edde, a huge fan of the Festival, helped out in the office on a voluntary year-round basis. Later, Elinor Workman would help off and on, mainly in the few months before and after the Festival.

When asked about his decision to leave the Festival, David noted that it seemed like it was time. The Festival at the time was in constant motion, with attendance practically doubling with each new year. "It was like the Wild, Wild West," he noted. "With more people came new challenges. It was challenging and exciting at the same time," he recalls.

He remembers one year when the then-ticket chairperson decided that it might be a good idea to give placard-type tickets as people came into the Festival. That way, they could wear them on their neck, and it would be easy to identify people that didn't have a ticket and shouldn't be at the Festival. "The problem was that as an attendee was leaving, they would give their placard ticket to someone waiting in line. And that person could enter the Festival free. It turned into a real nightmare," David said.

In retrospect, he notes that "the changing of chair positions—every two years—was a strength and a weakness for the Association. It was a strength, but a chair would every so often decide to change something without thinking it through, then it became a weakness."

A couple of issues he recalled were 1) keeping the ticket price the same over a number of years, as there was a real issue when it became necessary to increase the price, and 2) traffic and parking were always problematic.

His fond memories included his experiences with all the Presidents. "They were all great. Everyone was so energetic. It was all so new, and there were so many successes when I was Director." He has fond memories of the Victory Parties after the Festival, initially at Digger Dan's and then at the Barn on the Ranch side of Christmas Hill Park later on. He also mentioned the Thank You Dinner's that the Association put on for the volunteers: a mini Gourmet Alley held at Christmas Hill Park a few weeks after the Festival. "Volunteers were always the lifeblood of the Festival, and the early boards knew it."

David noted one of the big successes happened in Tim Filice's year with the development of the Man Hour concept that has been the backbone of the Association's mission ever since.

David has lived in Pleasanton with his wife, Cathy and daughter Isabel (age 23) since 1998.

Edith Edde, Hospitality Chairperson
Volunteer Office Assistant 1981-2018

Edith Edde was head of hospitality during the Festival's founding years. "When I was in charge, there were fewer volunteers," she noted in 2003. "Our job was to bring the food out to the workers, even those in the dusty parking lot. Edith served as a volunteer staff assistant in the Festival office between the years 1981 and 2018. She served on the Advisory Board in 1981 and 1982, and the Board of Directors in 1983 (Secretary) and again in 1985 (Director).

Elinor Workman
Multiple Years
Volunteer Office Helper

Associate Members

Associate members have this distinction because of their specific expertise and skill sets—essential to the Festival's success. There initially were two Associate members in the Festival Association—Bill Christopher (Garlic Topping) and Bonnie Gillio (Garlic Braiding). In 2001, Bonnie retired and handed over the duties of Garlic Braiding to Elaine Bonino.

In 2007, the Board of Directors added a third associate member, Bill Childers (Information Technology)—a membership that was only in place for a few years). In 2010, the Board of Directors approved an Associate membership for Promotions, Kat Filice. Her firm, Articulate Solutions, was then hired to handle promotions and marketing for the Festival.

Bill Christopher, Managing Partner of Christopher Ranch holds the distinction of having served the Garlic Festival for 41 years in the capacity of chair of the ever-popular garlic topping. In that capacity he has helped attendees learn about what happens to garlic once harvested.

Bonnie Gillio made her first garlic braid in 1972. "It's like French braiding hair," she said. She taught the Festival attendees how to braid from the first Festival in 1979 to 2000. "Besides being decorative, braided garlic keeps longer (about a year) because the top is still on, so air does not get into the head or stock," she added. In 1991, Gillio shipped her finished products across the country and as far away as Australia.

Garlic Theme Song Recorded

Local musician, Frank Mendiola recorded a country western tune "Sing a Song of Garlic" (the Garlic National Anthem) and a flip side rap song "What's That Smell" with Gary Steinmetz. The songs were a big hit at the 1981 Festival and the crowds quickly picked up on the tune and hummed along when they played them on the amphitheater stage.

GILROY'S THE ONE

Garlic can save you and I know it true
From cancer, high blood pressure, arthritis too
Garlic helped build the great pyramids
It also built Gilroy and we're glad it did
Chorus

The men here are stronger the women so fine
Kept young n pretty by south county wine
Your health is insured when you're livin' in our town
Breathing those fumes that come from the ground
Chorus

Trains n' trucks whistle as they scream on by
Tuned into KFAT there's no question why
Cowboys find Halls at the bucking horse
Gamblers find Garcia's it's a step game of course
Chorus

Drive just a little save a whole lot
Great deals in Gilroy aren't all we've got
Nob Hill brings produce the best in the land
The well is pure pleasure at Digger Dan's
Chorus

Low riders cruise their pride on the mall
And we all tip our hats to the Old City Hall
Our prunes n' tomatoes are part of our pride
We're number one Gilroy we can't be denied
Chorus

CHORUS

So, sing a song to garlic
Sing a song of life

Sing a song to Gilroy
with the children and wife

Join in the chorus
the recipe is strong

The garlic you love It
will make you live long

Gilroy's the one—
Gilroy's the one

For Garlic you love,
Gilroy's the one

The Board of Directors

Norie Goforth
Vice-President

Edith Edde
Secretary

Carl Swank
Treasurer

Tim Filice
President

Bill Ayer
Past President

Don Christopher
Director

Hy Miller
Director

Tim Filice was the first chair of Gourmet Alley, which was conceived for the second Festival in 1980. He recalls the frantic pace the Festival had in those early years when it was still evolving as the nation's premier cuisine gathering.

"I guess the single most significant impression I have is that we were flying by the seat of our pants in the early years," noted Filice. "We were constantly underestimating the response. We were amazed at the increasing number of people coming in."

"We were always scrambling around," he said. "Seems like 2 o'clock on Saturday we would be scouring every grocery store and supermarket in the county and San Benito County for butter and other ingredients."

"Those were exciting years because you didn't know what to expect," he said. "We were always in reactive mode, amazed by the number of people showing up. It was great fun in those early years."

The Festival has given Gilroy a lot more than just financial stability for non-profits and a sense of pride in the local garlic heritage. It has been a "learning seminar" in management and organization for many of the local citizens who have participated, Filice said.

"Those organizational skills, the (volunteers) take with them back to their organizations, be it Gilroy Gators (Swim Team) or the Elks or whatever," he said. "It's taught people how to put on events small and large. It's an organizational skill that they developed here. There are many people here who know how to get things done in terms of organization."

It has also provided local organizations with a dynamic networking resource.

"This community has a way of getting things done," he said. "And you know if you have a challenge, you want to put on an event here or raise money, immediately a shortlist of people comes to mind. You know who to call."

As a Festival pioneer, Filice played an important role in expanding it to include the Ranch Side part of Christmas Hill Park. It was an agricultural field at the time—dusty and teaming with insects.

Volunteers are necessary for the Festival's future, Filice said, and it's vitally essential for the event's success to make sure they're happy contributing, or they won't come back the following year.

"You could never afford to put on this event and pay people to do it," he said.

Attendance

110,000

What Was New

Third Attendance Day Added

Festival Expanded to Ranch Side

Danny Kaye Visited the Festival

$133,600 given to 92 Non-Profits

Parking Availability Increased

Queen Liz Archer

INTERESTING TIDBIT —

The Beginning of Official Volunteer Man Hours

Recognizing the importance of volunteers to the success of the Festival, a committee came up with an "all-for-one and one-for-all" plan where the volunteers in the massive food tent, Gourmet Alley, would split the total profits for their non-profit organizations based on man-hour time. The idea would later spread to incorporate all of the Festival volunteers.

Queen Liz Archer

[8 In the News]

Open Tennis Tourney Draws Top-Notch Players

The third annual event hosted 144 players who vied for singles and doubles titles. There were fewer returning champions, however, due to an out-of-state event staged at the same time. As a result, there were just 19 entrants in the women's field.

Local men's champion, Marcus Hughes, was out of the country and was not on hand to defend his crown. And last year's women's champion, Pascale Mato, was visiting here from France when she entered the tournament and didn't return in 1982.

Top seeds Janice Filice and Nancy Braughton, both from Gilroy, were in the finals of the women's intermediate women's singles.

Fourth Annual Garlic Festival 10K Run

Entrants came from as far as Illinois for the fourth annual 10,000 meter race. It was ran by 752 runners and the weather was comfortable for the race. A coin toss decided the winner as the two top runners crossed the finish line in a dead heat.

The **Garlic County Bike Tour**, later to be known as the Tour de Garlique, was introduced. The Garlic Festival hosted a bike tour from 1982 to 1999.

An Extra Day and More Space Added

A third day was added to the Festival event calendar, increasing the opportunity for locals concerned about the big crunch on Saturday and Sunday to enjoy the Festival. Locals were encouraged to attend the Festival either on Friday or first thing on Sunday morning.

Expanding the grounds to the Ranch side of Christmas Hill Park meant that Festival goers would have more ease of movement as they moved around the Festival.

In addition, those who choose to drive to the Festival found parking more accessible. The parking site could now accommodate some 80,000 to 85,000 cars, increasing dramatically from 1981 with a 23,000 capacity. Caltrans, the California Highway Patrol, and the city police department were in place to direct vehicles in and out of parking areas.

Gateway Center Thanks Committee

A huge "thank you" card was sent to the Garlic Festival committee, specially prepared by a group of sheltered youngsters whose lives, for a few hours, were touched by the Festival.

Made with the aid of teachers Steve Fortino and Debbie Italiano, the card bears paint hand prints of developmentally disabled children from Gateway Center for the Handicapped. The children ranged in ages from 4 to 13 years, with all but one of the children confined to a wheelchair.

Although only two could speak, Fortino said he felt they all enjoyed the Festival. When asked how he knew, he said, "sometimes it's a smile, a laugh, or just widening their eyes. We try to stimulate their senses. That's very important."

The Board of Directors

John Blaettler
Vice-President

Edith Edde
Secretary

Ken Cooper
Treasurer

Norie Goforth
President

Carl Swank
Past President

Janice Filice
Director

Jon Voorhies
Director

Even before the Festival's creation, **Norie Goforth** was well established in Gilroy's garlic industry. When she was president, she was sales manager at local garlic producer Christopher Ranch. For seven years, her husband, Leo, also got involved with the Festival, in charge of the pepper steak sandwiches–the most popular dish at Gourmet Alley.

The selling of merchandise was part of the evolution of the 1983 Festival as organizers that year, for the first time, allowed artisans and craftspeople to sell items incorporating garlic themes and high-quality products. The concept created another attraction and Festival tradition for guests other than food and entertainment.

Various off-site public events added to the fun of the Festival. Events like the "Garlic Squeeze Barn Dance" attracted country-music fans to the Christopher Ranch warehouse to hear the Billy Lawrence Band play such hits as "Okie from Muskogee."

Discontinued several years later, the annual dance was held the weekend before the Festival. Goforth remembered it fondly and in 2003 wished it might return as a Festival tradition. "It got the momentum rolling in the community for the Festival," she said.

Another event was Gilroy's version of the Tour de France. The Tour de Garlique was a bicycle tour through South County and San Benito County that drew 501 bikers. And more than 1,000 people ran in the Garlic Gallop, a 10-kilometer run starting at Gavilan College.

In all, more than 2,000 volunteers helped to make the Festival a success.

J. Chris Mickartz, Patty Filice, and Tim Filice.

Bob Miller and Paul Filice.

Attendance

104,622

What Was New

Added Country Stage—Four Stages

Arts & Crafts First Year

Tour de Garlique Debut

Rapazzini's Garlic Wine got National Attention

Queen Lauretta Barsi

The Year of the Media

Coverage was Overwhelming

Admission

$4 for adults and $2 for seniors and children. Opening day of the Festival, seniors and children were admitted for $1.

Gourmet Alley

Dish prices ranged from $1.50 to $4. A ton and a half of garlic was used for the Alley's seven-dish menu in 1983. Sales of dishes were up 40 percent compared with the previous year. The Alley's total sales were $485,000.

INTERESTING TIDBIT —

Garlique, the Talk of the Festival

A perfume, Garlique, was made from the essence of the city's favorite crop. A Cupertino-based firm, Scentsational Products, created the scent which was the most talked about item at the Festival in 1983. Gilroy resident Herman Garcia, working in the Garlique sales booth, described the perfume in a 1983 Dispatch article as "the thing to wear to the barbecue. It's also guaranteed to keep the vampires away."

Volunteers Are What Made Garlic Festival Beer Booths a Success

(From Gilroy Chamber of Commerce Business Focus dated September 1, 1983)

Smiling faces were the impression Garlic Festival visitors received as they approached the Chamber of Commerce beer booths. Those smiles paid off handsomely, for they helped the organization sell a record 20,577 gallons of beer during the three-day event. Manning the booths were more than 450 volunteers, and their enthusiasm for the job is seen in these photos. The same willingness to help visitors was seen in the booths operated by Chamber members throughout the Festival grounds. The Chamber Board of Directors owes the volunteers a hearty vote of thanks for their work. That work resulted in a net return of more than $66,000 to the organization.

Beer Booth volunteers "talk" up their booth to attract customers.

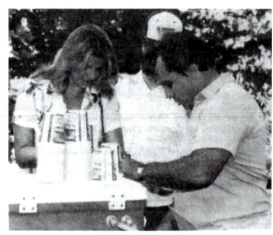
Bobby Fortino of Bottomley Distributing Company teaching beer pouring.

Supervisor Susan Wilson and Chamber Director Janis Bolt.

Enthusiastic volunteers joined in the fun.

Even Councilman Don Gage took a turn at the spigot.

Beer Booth funds were the responsibility of: Phil Skiver, Bill McIntosh, Don Smejdir, Karen Pogue and Brad Smith.

Don Nelson, on duty as booth boss.

Vern Gwinn, a Chamber Past President is seen on duty at base station operated by the Amateur Radio Operators Club.

Herman Garcia offers Garlic Festival queen and princess a sample of Garlique perfume.

Bobby Bonds and Tim Connelly watch Bob Infelise sink a putt on the sixth green at the Garlic Festival Golf Tournament.

12 Minute Bruschetta Recipe Wins Cook-Off

Neil Mahoney arrived late and breathless at the Garlic Festival recipe contest competition at Gavilan College. His brand-new car had acted up during his 900-mile trip to Gilroy from his home near Seattle, Washington.

But that didn't keep him from whipping out a dish of crispy French bread and cream sauce that won the hearts and taste buds of the judges, hands down. "It was unanimous," said an impressed Marion Burros, food reporter for the New York Times and author of seven cookbooks.

The judges included Burros; Green Grocer, Joe Carcione; Contra Costa Times food editor, Maggie Crum; Family Weekly food editor, Marilyn Hansen; Chicago Sun-Times food writer, Sharon Sanders; and KPIX Fireman-Chef, Jim Neil, from People are Talking.

The prize took home the $200 prize and the honor of wearing the official Cook-Off crown of garlic.

Mahoney's Bruschetta

Yield: 6 servings

1	loaf French or Italian bread, approx.12 inches long and 2 to 3 inches thick (sour dough is too salty!)
10	large cloves fresh garlic, peeled
½	cup olive oil
½	cup whipping cream
½	cup grated Locatelli (or Romano) cheese
½	cup Parmesan cheese
3	tbsp. unsalted butter
1	tbsp. chopped parsley

Cut bread diagonally in one-inch slices, without cutting through bottom crust. In food processor or blender, chop garlic fine with steel blade and add olive oil with processor running to make a thin paste. Slather garlic paste on cut surfaces and on top and side crusts of bread. Place in 350° oven, directly on rack (with pan on shelf below to catch drippings), and bake for 10 to 12 minutes, until top is crispy.

While the bread is in the oven, heat the cream in a heavy saucepan. Do not boil. Stir in the Romano and Parmesan slowly so that the sauce is absolutely smooth (a wire whisk works well). Stir in the butter and keep the sauce warm until the bread is ready.

When everyone is seated at the table, place the bread in a warm, shallow serving dish with sides. Cut through the bottom crust and poor the sauce over the bread. Sprinkle with the parsley and paprika and serve immediately.

The Board of Directors

Leonard Hale
Vice-President

Karen Christopher
Secretary

Mary Mozzone
Treasurer

Bob Dyer
Director

Ken Cooper
Director

Bill Reimal
Director

John Blaettler
President

A Certified Public Accountant **John Blaettler** had been involved with the Festival since its first year in various aspects, but mainly the finance area. He served as the finance chairman for two years and volunteered in the Gilroy Rotary, Gilroy Foundation, and St. Joseph's Family Center.

"I got on the (Festival) board for a couple of years and then became president," he recalls. "At that point, we were tweaking various aspects of (the Festival)—improving the parking and fine-tuning various aspects of it and expanding and improving the quality of the booths."

The only real snag he remembers was some challenges in closing down on Sunday evening. "But that didn't detract from the overall success."

As seen through an accountant's eyes, the Festival is quite an undertaking, so it's amazing how it always comes off every year. One way of looking at the Garlic Festival is as a corporation made up of more than 4,000 workers who come together for three days each year, set up the Festival infrastructure, and entertain about 125,000 guests from around the world. And somehow, despite the inevitable unexpected glitches, it always comes through.

"I think one of the greatest things they did, in the beginning, was the way they structured the leadership and the requirement of turnover for the chairs coming through the Festival," Blaettler said. "And I think they seem to be progressing forward in a great way in managing and attracting more people and getting people to come back."

The required turnover of leadership is essential in minimizing burn-out, he said. And the Festival association's strategic planning group, made up of past presidents, provides wisdom-from-experience advice that keeps the planning consistent with the spirit of the event.

The third ingredient for success is the high quality the Festival demands in what it offers guests, Blaettler said.

"I think the quality of the Festival they put on and the quality of the vendors and the entertainment they attract is critical," he said. "I think the great job they've done with quality and security issues, making sure there aren't problems with safety and gangs, makes people feel safe about coming."

As with any major event, sound financial planning is crucial to ensure the long-term life of the Festival, he said.

"They're incredibly strong," he said of the Festival's finances.

"They (the Festival association) have gone through some downturns in the economy. They've had downturns in attendance. But they have a strong reserve to protect themselves for the future. They're always looking at things they can improve financially."

A significant part of the Festival's draw is that the volunteers have a good time there, and their lively spirit creates a fun time for the crowds.

"It's being part of a big party," he said. "There's a lot of comradeship because people like working with the same people year after year."

INTERESTING TIDBIT —

National Flag at Festival

John Albaugh, a local Gilroy community leader, was asked by his best friend Joe Silva of Los Banos, why there wasn't an American flag flown at the Festival. John went to the City Offices and asked that a flag be flown at the event. A pole was installed and the flag was flown not only for the Festival but for other community events at Christmas Hill Park. Joe and John were both veterans of WWII.

(See top photo of dedication ceremony held at the Gazebo Stage on page 44.)

Attendance
125,000

What Was New
Parked Some 25,000 cars
ShaBoom added to Entertainment Venue

Special Recognition
Bob Skillma, Howard Alexander, Albino Moretti Jr. and Nick Zuckowski

Queen Janet Orgill (McAllister)

Garlic Gallop Was His First Race; but Not His Last

(Based on special submitted to The Dispatch by Lynn Viale, Freelance Writer)

Andy Viale

Just five weeks before the Festival, Andy Viale turned 40, ran his first mile, and gave up smoking cigars.

When he described the pleasure of running down pastoral Santa Teresa Boulevard to his wife, Lynn, she said, "Don't be surprised if you see 600 runners coming at you from the opposite direction tomorrow. The Gilroy Garlic Gallop starts at 7:30 in the morning."

A light went on in Andy's head — "Do you think I could do it, too? Run 6.2 miles? With all those people around?" She assured him that he could undoubtedly gallop that distance if he set his mind to it.

So the following day, with nerves as taut as if he had been heading for the Olympics,

he assured Lynn that his fear was not of the running but "the fear of 7-year-olds passing him."

By 6 am, they were at Gavilan. Andy didn't want to be late for his first race, so allowing an hour and a half for the two-minute ride to Gavilan just made sense.

No one knew Andy was a novice unless they heard him ask what a 10K was. And his comment: "Look at all those joggers" raised an eyebrow or two among the "runners."

In two minutes under one hour, Andy came puffing to the finish line. Beaming, he gulped his Calistoga water and announced, "Now, I am (gasp, gasp!) a runner!"

FAR LEFT:
Kyla Garnett with her dad.

LEFT:
Local tennis celebrity, Marcus Hughes

Festival's First Bride and Groom

Tom and Wendy Aiello came all the way from San Diego so they could enjoy the Garlic Festival and get married—at the same time.

Judge Joseph Biafore Jr. of Gilroy pronounced the couple man and wife in a ten minute ceremony that ended with the Garlic Queen presenting the bride with a garlic braid.

Our Town is Us This Weekend

Partial Excerpt

from an editorial

in The Dispatch

by Huck Hagenbuch

Warmly wonderful. Hotly hectic. It's that time again when Gilroy hosts the world, and to tell the truth, Garlic Festival is ranking right up there with Christmas as a highlight of the year.

Now we get to pay back some of the riches that living in Gilroy offers. The riches of close friendships; people who really mean it when they say "How are You?" Riches of running into a friend in town and stopping to visit for half an hour when seconds before you were in a rush to get somewhere else.

John Young is right. The quality of life in this town is one of the best in the world. The essence of this fact may be exuded from our people as the essence of garlic exudes from our soil every summer. That must be at least part of the reason people keep coming back to our party year after year.

Paying back the riches is an honor, one we accept in return for being a focal point of attention for a weekend.

Visitors talking about the Festival use a lot of adjectives. Notice sometime how few are normally used in conversation. We communicate efficiently, for the most part, and descriptive words are sacrificed to brevity. But when someone is talking about the Festival, you can see them shift into a

slower gear, roll back the head, and the adjective file comes into focus.

Words like "mellow" come out. "Kicked back." "Marvelous." "Greatest event of the year." "Fantastic." Superlatives abound. Become commonplace. Are glazed in the sugary nostalgia of the party that is the Festival.

You know these folks haven't come to Gilroy from hundreds and thousands of miles away because of the wide, tree-lined streets, or the small town atmosphere. Most of them don't even see our town except maybe for Tenth Street or Leavesley and then into a parking lot.

So, if it's not our town that's bringing people here it must be the folks of the town. It must be something like the friendly, laid-back attitude we have about hosting our party, at least externally. It may be the sun-tanned, orange-shirted people of our town guiding visitors to parking places, baking in the sun and smiling and having a great time in spite of the heat and the dust.

We can be extremely proud of our town this weekend. Our town is us. And the Festival is every third one of us working to help make it what it is, with the other two-thirds supporting the operation.

That's Gilroy.

'ShaBoom' Wows Festival Goers with Good Old-time Rock'n'roll

Dan Quinet of the San Jose band 'ShaBoom' belts out "Jailhouse Rock" and other early rock tunes for a dancing and cheering audience at the Christmas Hill amphitheater. They would go on to play each year of the Festival until 2008 when they retired.

The Board of Directors

John Locey
Vice-President

Ernest Filice, Jr.
Secretary

Karen Christopher
Treasurer

Leonard Hale
President

Edith Edde
Director

Mary Mozzone
Director

Richard Mackie
Director

The Festival began to gain national and international exposure with camera crews coming from as far away as Germany and Japan to video-tape it for their audiences, **Leonard Hale** remembers. During the 1985 Festival, the media exposure was unending.

"We did a lot of television talk shows and stuff like that," he said. "Someone was on the talk shows all the time. … National Geographic came and did a bunch of pictures and stuff but we never got into the magazine."

One problem with the Festival in 1985 was learning to deal with the flow of traffic for the thousands of guests, Hale remembers. The Festival board had decided to end the event on a high note by having the best bands play late Sunday afternoon and this caused a highly-congested traffic jam of guests.

"We realized that was a little tricky," Hale recalls. "Everyone who wanted to get out of the Festival went against people going to the amphitheater. There was just not enough room."

But the problems of those early years provided learning experiences that made the Festival a much smoother-running experience now, he said.

Hale started out his Garlic Festival involvement in the parking lot the first year when organizers contracted with the Gilroy Jaycees to do parking.

"That was a tough job," he said, describing how dusty and hot it could get in the parking fields. "And then you see some of the people doing it now and they weren't even around the first year …

"When I was the chairman of the parking committee, parking took care of both the traffic and the parking. We got

everyone that could help. The Highway Patrol put their five or six people there to help out. But it just became overwhelming for everyone. So we turned to the Highway Patrol in Sacramento and wrote a contract for CHP officers to deal with traffic.

"And with grass drying in the hot July sun, there was always a fire in the parking lot. People would drop cigarettes or automobile catalytic converters would ignite the grass. One year, the weeds started to combust around cars parked over them and the fire spread quickly burning a few autos.

"We replaced a little bit of wiring and fixed up a couple of cars, it was nothing major," Hale said. "From that time on we had a fire truck in the parking lot."

Attendance

137,000

What Was New

First Art Poster

Cook Off moved to Festival Grounds

$219K was given to 112 Non-Profits Organizations and Charities bringing the total for the first seven years to $1 Million.

Volunteer of the Year

Mike Griffis

Queen Monica Baca

INTERESTING TIDBIT —

Fame and Fortune Strikes

The 1985 Festival received exposure on a TV variety show produced by Dick Clark Productions. The star of the show was filmed running backwards on the garlic run. When the tape was run in reverse, it showed him running ahead as everyone else going the other way… a hilarious effect.

Art Poster by John Park

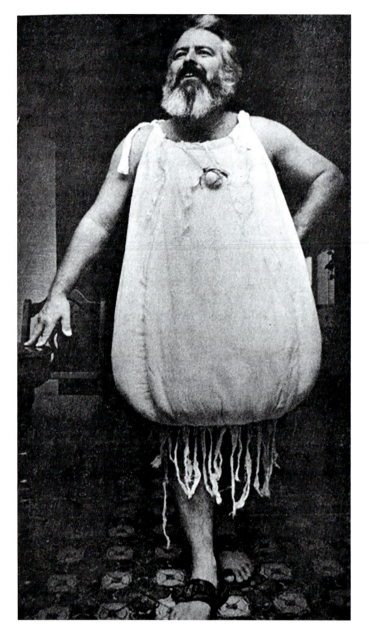

Mr. Garlic, Al Hansen in Official Greeter Role

During the Festival, Al Hansen was on call throughout each of the three days for photographs, jokes, and general carousing. He wears a pair of sandals and dons 25 pounds of unbleached muslin and cotton batting to get into his Mr. Garlic character.

But it wasn't until he had those six oversized cloves gathered around his waist, a crown of bulbs on his head, leaves sprouting from his shoulders, and a fringe of roots at his fee that he felt inspired by the herb.

"Once a year for three days, I get to be somebody else. I feel happy. I go around welcoming people and getting my photo taken with them. I get to hug the girls; I get all the beer I can drink and free food."

Though Hansen says he loves the attention, the job does have its hazards, and he tries to bear them with grace. His suit gets a little hot, and he can't sit down, or the cloves would crumble in his lap. After three days of the Festival, the white muslin can become quite filthy. And since no dry cleaner would touch the suit, Hansen's wife, Martha, made a new one every year.

Martha Hansen was as much a hand in the success of Mr. Garlic as the big bulb himself. She took two full days to make the suit and improved on its design each year since Bob Kraemer wore the suit at the first Garlic Festival in 1979.

Artist Unknown

Kraemer's suit was similar to the one Martha makes for Al—except she noted that it didn't "bulb out" quite right. She then put elastic at the bottom of the suit and took extra care to stuff and sew each clove separately to get the appropriate effect.

When in Gilroy, Do as Gilroyans Do

Described by practitioners as a useful and decorative way to store garlic, braiding can also be a sometimes frustrating test of manual dexterity. The popular braiding lessons were offered all three days of the Festival.

Bonnie Gillio of Gillio Farms in Hollister taught out-of-towners how all good Gilroyans braid their garlic.

1985
Garlic Festival
Archive Photos

The Board of Directors

Glenn Suyeyasu
Vice-President

Rita Timewell
Secretary

Don Crowther
Treasurer

John Locey
President

Ernest Filice Jr.
Director

Robert Miller
Director

Arlene Livorsi
Director

John Locey, the Festival's president in 1986, worked as a facilities supervisor at Gilroy Foods, now Olam International.

"The weather was great. It was typical Gilroy, not overly hot," he remembers. "It was the 'See America' year, which was part of what attracted the crowds."

"See America" was the theme the United States travel industry created that year to promote domestic vacationing.

The Festival was still growing and undergoing its evolution. And it was very popular at the time because it was so novel, and everyone wanted to see what it was all about, Locey said.

"There were a few issues, but you will have some issues with that many people attending," he said. "Our biggest thing back then was getting through the weekend. Every year until 1987, the attendance kept getting bigger and bigger, so we were uncertain what to plan for."

The number of Festival attendees eventually leveled off helping future presidents know how many guests to expect. Locey said that would make things much easier to plan.

The Ranch Site at that time was just dirt, and there was concern about the condition for guests.

"We had to go in and prepare that," Locey said. "We planted grass down there and tried different things to keep the dust down."

Locey's 12-year-old daughter, Shannon, helped out at the Festival and had a good time. And among the many Festival guests were the old-time movie stars, Phil Harris and Alice Faye, a married couple who came to sample the garlic cuisine.

"They were very genuine people," Locey recalls.

Locey worked at every Festival since the first one in 1979. He remembers setting up booths at the Bloomfield Ranch site and helping with the parking that year.

Being president in 1986 was busy, but he was grateful both personally and professionally for the experience.

"I think the Festival helps me in my personal and business achievements," he said. "Working with the people and the size of the budget you're dealing with, it's a huge benefit for me. The Festival is part of me. I've been doing it for 25 years. It's a great thing. It's hard to put what goes back into the community and how it brings the community together into words. You just don't see that anywhere else." 🧄

Attendance
142,000

What Was New
Ronald McDonald in Children's Area

Volunteer of the Year
Lou Fiori

Queen Franca Barsi

INTERESTING TIDBIT —

Dick Nicholls was hired as Executive Director of Festival.
(See page 103,148)

Art Poster by Scott Lance & Tommy Gibson

LEFT: Godfather of Garlic Festival, Val Filice waves as he works his magic in Gourmet Alley.
ABOVE: Garlic Festival workers prepare loaves of garlic bread to be sold.

World's Media Still Singing Festival Praises

There is a time every year when thousands of Americans and visitors go ga-ga over garlic.
For this is the occasion of the Great Garlic Festival.

Lim Ching HIng, New Straits Times (11/14/85)

The **New Straits Times**, an English-language newspaper serving Kuala Lumpur, Malaysia was just one of dozens of overseas news organizations that had dispatched reporters to cover the Festival in the first seven years.

In the US, the Festival had received play in **The Christian Science Monitor, The Washington Post**, the **Chicago Sun-Times**, and the **St. Louis Post Dispatch**. And most notable of print media in 1986 was the coverage in **USA Today**.

The headline read **"Aroma Swirls in Gilroy…Pungency pays off for this old California town."** The article goes on to say: Gilroy boasts two of the world's largest fresh-garlic operations, including the A&D Christopher Ranch,

which handles 20 million pounds of garlic a year; two of the largest processors, which chop, peel and pulverize 60 million pounds; and the biggest garlic party of all, drawing 130,000 people and $350,000 in profits.

But the media coverage was not confined to print media. The Festival was featured in a segment of **TV's Bloopers and Practical Jokes**. And on the television quiz show, **Jeopardy**, contestants were asked what is celebrated at Gilroy's annual Festival.

Although no cash was spent on advertising, the Garlic Festival enjoyed plenty of exposure around the world via the printed and broadcast word.

Delta and **PSA** airline passengers read about the Festival in flight

magazines in the spring. On the ground, readers in Seattle, Chicago and Milbourne, Florida read about the Festival in newspapers.

Some free tickets were given to radio stations in Stockton, Sacramento and Napa Valley. Listeners in those areas were exposed to the Festival that way.

The Festival also had plenty of coverage locally. **KICU-TV**, a San Jose station seen on **Channel 36**, sent cameras to broadcast live 30-to-60-second vignettes six to ten hours a day on Saturday and Sunday.

KHIP-FM radio, at 93.5 on the dial, also did live broadcasts with reports from the Festival at least once each hour on Saturday and Sunday.

Festival's First Trip to Japan

In 1987, a group of wealthy Japanese businessmen financed a trip to Japan. The intent was to set the foundation for a Japanese Cultural Center in the foothills east of Gilroy. The center never happened but a long-term relationship with Takko Machi, Gilroy 's Sister City, was established.

The ten-day trip was organized by local businessman, Ted Uchida, and included among others the 1987 Garlic Festival Queen, Jennifer Stoughton (Speno), her chaperone, Andrea Habing, Glenn Suyeyasu, 1987 Festival President, Garlic Festival Director, Dave Bouchard, and Gilroy Mayor, Roberta Hughan.

The extraordinary trip was memorialized by Mayor Roberta Hughan who gathered reflections and photos from all ten participants and presented them to Ted Uchida in a typically Japanese book. Ted describes it as one of his most prized possessions.

... at the Institute of Moralogy

... at the Prince Hotel

... at the Ranch

... in Nagasaki

... at the Reception

浪漫草子

Gourmet Alley

UPPER LEFT (l-r): Brad Smith and Bob Miller cooking scampi.

UPPER RIGHT (l-r): Jason Valenta and Matthew Hussar man the stir fry pan.

FAR LEFT: Kay Carlson (middle) with her sister Bonnie (left) and Kristy Ferraro (back left) prepping vegetables.

LEFT: Diane Scariot rests between shifts.

Garlic Express
Prototype of Rail Transit to Gilroy

1987
Garlic Festival
Archive Photos

The Board of Directors

John Parrinello
Vice-President

Andrea Habing
Secretary

Paul Filice
Treasurer

Gregg Giusiana
President

Larry Mickartz
Director

Rich Freedman
Director

Bob Miller
Director

Security and traffic were **Gregg Giusiana**'s fields of expertise. But, in 1988, he stepped out of his police shoes and into the highly esteemed role of president during the Garlic Festival's 10th anniversary year.

"I remember the very first board meeting I attended. I was elected vice president and had no clue what I was getting into," Giusiana said.

As the traffic committee chairman, Giusiana spent most of his time making sure cars were moving along smoothly in and out of town. And, because his prior position wasn't on Festival grounds, he had not spent much time there. So, he had a lot to learn and subsequently would ask questions like, "Where is the information booth?"

"I had to spend my year as vice president learning about all the different operations at the Festival," he said. "I dragged myself from one area of the Festival to another, asking questions — to learn everything before I became president."

"This Festival has given Gilroy a name," he said. "You can't go anywhere without running into someone who hasn't heard about or been to the Festival, and that is something to be proud of."

One of the goals Giusiana strove to achieve was contacting past directors and presidents, asking them to come back and give their advice and expertise— forming the strategic planning committee.

"The founding fathers' wisdom is the basis for why the Festival runs so smoothly," Giusiana said. "I think it is very important to keep knowledgeable people around for their advice and expertise on how things should run."

Along with the founders, past presidents, board members, and volunteers got a chance to meet with old and new faces weeks before the 10th anniversary Festival.

"It was a great way for all the people who helped to get to know each other," Giusiana said.

At the same time that he was gathering advice and strategies from the old, Giusiana stressed the importance of bringing in the new.

"Having new chair members every two years keeps the Festival from becoming stale, and because the Festival gives so much back to the community, it keeps the volunteer base intact," he said.

Tom White
Director

INTERESTING TIDBIT —

Wedding Bells Rang Once Again

Ellie Lindgren and Lynn Winters had their first date at the Festival and being garlic lovers, they decided to get married at the celebration that brought them together.

As Lindgren wore a veil donned with garlic, and Winters sported a bulb boutonniere, the couple happily strutted down the aisle Friday and started their very stinky honeymoon by perusing around the Festival.

10th Annual
Gilroy Garlic Festival
JULY 29 30 31 1988
Art Poster by Shirley Ng

The World-Famous Budweiser Clydesdales Visit the Garlic Festival

An elite team of high-stepping Clydesdales kicked-off the Garlic Festival, leading a parade through town to Christmas Hill Park. The Clydesdales were brought in from Southern California by Bottomley Distributing of Milpitas, the appearance paid for by Anheuser Busch.

Rich Mackie worked with Bottomley for four years, trying to get authorization for the visit. He stated that "management for the Clydesdales had strict rules regulating their performance—they're very pampered and they don't want them sitting out in the sun too long."

Clydesdales must be three years old, six feet at the shoulder and weigh between 1,800 and 2,300 pounds to be on the Budweiser team.

Giusiana said one of the highlights of his presidency was having the opportunity to welcome the one-millionth person into the Festival's gates.

"It was great," he said. "We gave him and his mother a VIP tour of the Festival, and it was even more special because it was the first time they had ever been."

"The Festival's formula is so good; it will be successful for a long time," he said. "One of the things that makes me sure of this is the workers' 'things can get done' attitude. Anytime an issue came up, there was always someone who said they could get it done." 🧄

A belt buckle vendor produced a limited edition buckle to celebrate the Festivals 10th Anniversary.

The Board of Directors

Sam Bozzo
Vice-President

Cindy Gettman
Secretary

Larry Mickartz
Treasurer

John Parrinello
President

Tim Filice
Director

Dave Peoples
Director

Andrea Habing
Director

In 1989, the Festival was still pretty young, and President **John Parrinello** felt fortunate to have a lot of input from the founding fathers.

"Don Christopher and Rudy Melone saw things through," he said. "In those days, our main concern was looking for things to improve each coming year."

One of the things Parrinello said improved during his term was the structure and organization of the association.

"It really wasn't my doing," he said. "The committees and the volunteers made this thing happen. They had such amazing dedication."

Another highlight of his presidency was the combined decision with the board to make the event more family-friendly. The Children's Area was put in place, the music schedule was mixed-up, and the beer availability was reduced, making the Festival attractive to a mixture of different people.

"We had groups of people in RVs camping out in the parking lot before the tents were even set up," he said.

Parrinello said people could go to any food Festival globally, but they come to the Garlic Festival to celebrate with people of common interests.

"Obviously, they come for the lure of garlic, but they also come because of the atmosphere," he said. "People here are always having a tremendous time, sharing common interests."

During his year of preparation, Parrinello noticed other communities commenting on the Festival's success.

"I would have members of other cities and Festivals approach me and ask, 'How do you guys do it?'" he said. "The unity of the residents to pull the Festival off makes Gilroy look like a good place to live."

Parrinello gave the most credit to the Festival's founders and said that things wouldn't have

John Young
Director

continued to be so successful without their support and guidance.

"I think the way chair positions change every two years keeps new blood and fresh ideas coming in," he said

Parrinello was the Pacific Gas and Electric manager in Gilroy for nine years. He transferred to Lake County, in the northwestern part of the state, where he retired in 1997. 🧄

Attendance
129,000

What Was New

Chilled-Water Dispensers
Children's Entertainment Area

$262K was given to 145 Non-Profits bringing the total for the eleven years to $2 Million.

Volunteer of the Year
Jim Gama (Utilities)

Special Recognition
Howard Alexander and Chuck Ogle

Queen Connie Temple

INTERESTING TIDBIT —

Happy Visitors Prove Less is More

A cooling breeze, newly shaded attractions and slightly smaller crowds comforted Gilroy Garlic Festival patrons so much that they reacted like happy consumers should — they spent more money. "Attendance was down a tiny bit, but it appears the money that was spent was up," said Victoria Klass at the Festival's conclusion on Sunday. "It wasn't as hot. Everyone was having a better time and it showed in the money they spent."

Gilroy Garlic Festival

July 28, 29, 30, 1989

Art Poster by Charlotte Yep

Facts and Figures
Festival XI, 1989

Gourmet Alley

Pepper Steak Sandwiches
15,103 pounds, 24,835 Servings

Calamari
7,500 pounds, 11,249 Servings

Scampi
12,046 Servings

Mushrooms
3,480 pounds, 15,547 Servings

Pasta Con Pesto
35,135 Servings
Pasta 5,560 pounds
Pesto 240 gallons

French Bread
77,760 Servings

Stir Fry Vegetables
4,802 Servings

Chili
3,922 Servings

Charcoal
5,500 pounds

Beer & Wine Sales

Beer
29,600 gallons, 316,277 Servings

Souvenir Glasses Sold
22,000

Wine
28,205 glasses Served

These figures reflect only the Festival Associations Gourmet Alley, Gilroy Chamber of Commerce Beer, and Rotary Wine Concessions. They do not include the 100 booths in the garlic themed marketplace.

[In the News]

Children's Area Takes Center Stage

The Children's area offered a new dimension to youngsters, who in times past had only a few strolling balloon vendors, clowns, and a stage that seemed almost an afterthought. In 1989, there were no questions that families were highly sought after, and their kids were as cherished as the parents' taste buds. There is a new designated area "for kids only," with booths, entertainment, and food appropriate to their likes. The site, which was half of the divided gazebo, was much more intimate and left no question that kids were a priority. The other side of the partition still served as a stage for adult entertainment.

Children's Area mural designed by (l-r) Maria Lalor, Karen Garnett and Judy King was co-sponsored by the Gilroy Chamber of Commerce and Hecker Pass, A Family Adventure. It was 8' high and 36" wide.

Disneyland's Mickey Mouse goofs around with the garlic "Bulbettes" during the Garlic Festival opening ceremonies.

Garlic Centipede members started an annual tradition of kicking up their heels at the 10K Run.

Gerry Foisy Takes over Mr. Garlic Job

Somewhere around 1988, Jeanne Foisy, who worked at Gilroy Foods, asked her husband, Gerry, if he would help out—helping out turned into coordinating all the people who worked as "Mr. Garlic," which turned into just being "Mr. Garlic."

The job turned into a goodwill mission for garlic, and "Mr. Garlic" has taken on almost cartoon reality. A quick Google search reveals hundreds of photos with "Mr. Garlic." In 2008, the Garlic Festival bobblehead doll was "Mr. Garlic."

The upside of his role as "Mr. Garlic" is the opportunity to meet and be photographed with people worldwide. Gerry has taken "Mr. Garlic" to numerous social events, benefits, and TV shows. The downside of his notoriety is being recognized on the street or in the store as "Mr. Garlic." Few people seem to know him by his real name!

Joanne Kraemer made the original costume. Since then, Dave Peoples and the Nimble Thimble have kept it "alive." Thanks to some friends of Gerry and Jeanne, the 2008 "Mr. Garlic" sprouted some small garlic cloves around the bottom of the costume. And the Festival's bobblehead doll was Mr. Garlic.

Jeanne, Gerry's wife, accompanied Gerry on his "Mr. Garlic" rounds. She knew how to operate all kinds of cameras and carried an ample supply of sunscreen and water.

Gerry Foisy was "Mr. Garlic" for 30 years. He retired in 2016.

The title of Mr. Garlic is a bloodline succession. "I got a letter from my son, and he said, 'I want to take your place," so I couldn't say no," Foisy said.

He was moved to tears. "It means a lot that he cared enough to say, 'I'm going to take your place.' So it was nice," he said.

The Board of Directors

Gene Sakahara
Vice-President

Pat Gewin
Secretary

Art Gillespie
Treasurer

Sam Bozzo
President

Tim Filice
Director

Tom White
Director

Cindy Gettman
Director

Rick Heinzen
Director

It was the year that the first Garlic Festival president was invited to visit Gilroy's sister city, Takko-Machi.

Sam Bozzo remembers being on a Delta Airlines flight to Japan in 1990. During the flight, he heard his own voice in a recorded interview on the public address system describing the Festival's attractions to the passengers. Later, Bozzo played a tape of that same interview at the Garlic Festival's annual meeting.

"For me, it told the story of how international we were," he said. "We have people from all over the world coming. With our involvement with Takko-Machi, we know people come from worldwide."

The Festival in 1990 attracted about 125,000 guests. The Gilroy Dispatch wrote the event had been "flawless," Bozzo remembers.

But there were a few hiccups to overcome. That year, the famous Garlic Train that brought visitors from San Francisco to the Garlic Capital had to be canceled, Bozzo said.

"One unfortunate thing was that we couldn't authorize the Garlic Train because of insurance," he said. "And that was unfortunate because it was such a great thing coming from San Francisco."

CalTrain wanted the Festival organization to pick up the first $100,000 in liability if a passenger got hurt and sued. That amount of money would take almost half the event's profits, and Bozzo didn't want to take the risk.

In 1990, Bozzo created public safety volunteers called "Garlic Angels," the name coming from the Guardian Angels, well-known for protecting citizens on the streets of urban areas.

He said that the Angels were mainly on the lookout for underage drinking problems if teenagers managed to sneak a drink.

"The idea was to help us with the yard duty. We had them wear pink shirts," he said. "In 2003, we had the Info folks (to look out for trouble), which I think is a better use of volunteers."

Bozzo has been involved with the culinary Festival since its first year. He and his wife Judy set up a booth that year selling garlic soup.

He laughs because the hot liquid might not have been an excellent choice to serve during the sweltering month of July. He ended up with about seven five-gallon buckets of soup. However, it did not go to waste.

He and his wife simply sold the soup at their restaurant, Digger Dan's.

Bozzo and his good friend Gene Sakahara, who served as president in 1991, have become the Ambassadors of Goodwill for the Festival. They travel to various other Festivals around America and Canada to demonstrate garlic cooking tips and recipes. They call themselves Team SakaBozzo and have a lively, light-hearted approach to entertain their audiences.

The team is even planning a garlic-oriented cookbook, calling it "Any Bozzo Can Cook," he said. "People keep asking when it's coming out. For the last seven years, it's coming out soon."

Attendance
125,000

What Was New
Up With People Traveling Troop Visited and Performed

Joann Kessler Joined the Festival Staff

Festival Queen Appeared in the Rose Parade

Children's Area was Expanded

Garlic Angels Created

Volunteer of the Year
Chuck Ogle (Refuse)

Queen Kim Yafai

Art Poster by Terry Wetmore

New Assistant Director Hired for Festival

Joann Kessler joined Dick Nicholls and Loyce Lombard in the Festival office.

Garlic Train Derailed

The popular Garlic Express was canceled due to a dispute with Southern Pacific over insurance. The line ran between San Francisco and Gilroy, stopping in Burlingame, Redwood City, Palo Alto and San Jose for the past three years. Up to 4,500 people avoided the traffic down Highway 101 by using this service.

Continued from page 75

Bozzo's year as president deepened the relationship that Gilroy had with the community of Takko-Machi. The Japanese town of about 8,000 people had made a tradition of paying for the Gilroy Garlic Queen to come and visit at its annual beef and garlic Festival. When Bozzo visited, he had a conversation with the mayor.

"What happened as a result of that? The mayor of that town wanted to develop some kind of creative position where a young person, a graduate of a college who grew up in Gilroy, would work somewhere in Takko-Machi."

The result was a new position, called coordinator of international relations, where a resident of Gilroy would live in the sister city for a year.

Bozzo's professional life away from garlic is serving as the Director of Personnel for the Monterey County Office of Education. He feels proud of Gilroy's status as the Garlic Capital.

"I don't think there's a day that goes by when I don't think about the Garlic Festival," he said. "In our family, it's been our life. We live it. To me, it's what brings our community together."

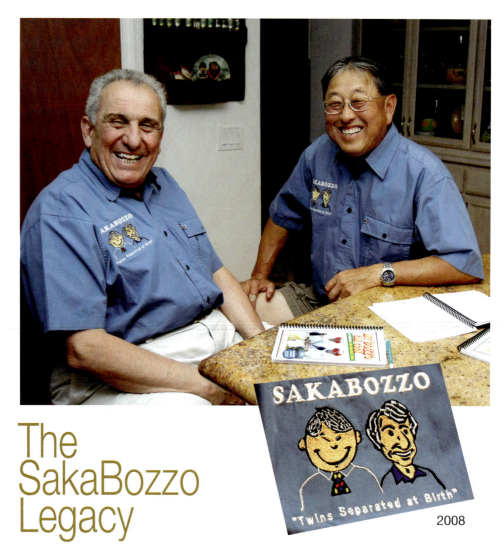

SAKABOZZO "Twins Separated at Birth" 2008

The SakaBozzo Legacy

There are all types of professionals, but these guys are hard to categorize. They are professional cookbook authors with a clever knack for making people laugh. The team of Gene Sakahara and Sam Bozzo aka, SakaBozzo, "Twins Separated at Birth." Although a fantastic pair of twins — in jest, they both come from two completely different worlds. Sam comes from a very Italian heritage, while Gene's ancestry is Japanese.

Their partnership roots, founded in the Garlic Festival — had just the right combination of chemistry and commonality. Both have served as the President of the Gilroy Garlic Festival — Sam Bozzo in 1990 and Gene Sakahara in 1991. Both are retired school district human resources administrators. They have a strong bond in laughter and often publicly trade barbs and banter. It all began in 1991 when they were both at "Super Market in the Park," at the then- private park of Nob Hill Foods, now Gilroy Gardens. Dr. Rudy Melone, a Gilroy Garlic Festival founder and the asso-

ciation's first President was scheduled to put on a cooking demonstration but took sick. Gene and Sam were asked to step in, and the team of SakaBozzo was born. They demonstrated traditional scampi and calamari dishes that day.

As the years have passed, their casual banter has grown into a comedic cooking duo act, and they have turned pro. Although they still do a lot of volunteer gigs, they also do many paid jobs. They get paid to have fun, cook, and entertain. Their routine has taken them to Canada, Japan, Del Rey Beach, Florida, and elsewhere in the US. They have performed cooking demonstrations for "A Taste of Home" and World Wide Tours. People from all over join in a three or four-day tour of cooking demonstrations. The SakaBozzo team was part of the "Taste of the Valley" tour.

Of course, not all their demonstrations have been as polished. Once, at the Rice Festival in Gridley, they had the honor of following Martin Yan, Yan Can

2007

Cook, the celebrated Chinese chef. They didn't realize that Yan brought his stove, utensils, and general kitchen paraphernalia and would take them with him when he left. So, they had to borrow utensils and prepare the meal over a white-gas camping stove!

As the team got more gigs, they tried to script the act, but they decided to go back to their barbs and banter after a few bombs. They were back to who they were, and success returned, or as they self describe it, "the trials and tribulations of a still-rising comedic cooking team." Over the years, they perfected their act.

Their first cookbook, Any Bozzo Can Cook, debuted at the Gilroy Garlic Festival in 2008. The book is a compilation of sixteen years of experimentation, eating, and having fun. The spectrum of recipes is exceptional — from Fried Baloney Sandwiches to Timballo di Maccherone

e Melanzane. The book has stories and some of the adventures of the "Twins Separated at Birth." If cookbooks are scary culinary puzzles, Any Bozzo Can Cook is a cook's cookbook motivated by "food, family, and fun."

In 2009, they added some recipes and came out with the second edition, and in 2018, their third cookbook has 68 more garlic-flavored masterpieces.

As "professional ambassadors" of the Gilroy Garlic Festival, Sam and Gene's Festival legacy spanned over 28 years. The aromatic artisans hung up their aprons after their final appearance on the Friday afternoon of the 38th Festival. For all those years, they have been one of the reasons the Garlic Festival had maintained its fun, family atmosphere despite its tremendous growth over the years.

Any **BOZZO**
Can Cook **III**

By SakaBozzo
Gene Sakahara & Sam Bozzo
TWINS SEPARATED AT BIRTH

Demo Chefs at the Gilroy Garlic Festival for 25 Years

2018

Critter Sightings Threaten to Add Additional Aroma to Festival

Several reports of busy-tailed mammals seen in the park, made some of the organizers a little on edge. Between two and six skunks were roaming the grounds; probably brought down from surrounding hills because of the drought. Bob Connelly, city parks director predicted the little guys would be no match for the garlic and 100.000-plus crowds that would descend on park.

Garlic Express Derailed

Train buffs and garlic lovers who liked to ride the rails to the Festival were disappointed as the popular runs for the weekend were canceled. For the past three years, the special Garlic Express ran on the Southern Pacific line between San Francisco and Gilroy, stopping in Burlingame, Redwood City, Palo Alto and San Jose.

Up to 4,500 people used the trains once the service was expanded in 1988 to include both weekend days, officials estimated. Contract negotiations failed over insurance liability issues.

Even the Local Newspaper — The Dispatch — Smelled

The Dispatch added garlic oil to the ink of the paper to create news for the nose. For the first time, The Dispatch smelled like the town it covered. "We thought it would be a fun way to promote the Garlic Festival," said Dispatch publisher Fuller Cowell. "We first thought of it a couple of years ago, but we never got it together until now."

[In the News]

From Festival Volunteers "Why do they do it!"

INFORMATION — Tony Taormino
"I thoroughly enjoy the feeling of camaraderie. I enjoy working with so many people that I know. It makes me proud to be from Gilroy when you see how many people come from so far away to participate."

PARKING — Sal Satterfield
"Working at the Garlic Festival gives me the opportunity to give something back to the community that gives so much to us."

SOUVENIRS — Pia Berryman
"I think that knowing the money is going to the community and the great spirit of community that is nurtured by working at the Garlic Festival is very important. It makes me feel comfortable and all warm and fuzzy inside."

GOURMET ALLEY — Bob McHam
"My wife and I have worked for the past 9 or 10 years. We do it because it feels so good when it's over. You work hard for a few days, but then you've helped so many people. It's a feeling of pride...to be part of a community like this one. Other towns have tried and failed to do what we do successfully every year."

GOLF TOURNAMENT — Gene Gewin
"The money we bring into the community is really needed. Whenever you can get that many people together to work towards a common goal it's amazing."

TICKETS — Anne Hepner
"I love the sense of community that is the Festival and the feeling of pride. I recommend that everybody jump at the opportunity to be a volunteer. I admire the dedication of all the volunteers."

FINANCE — Vince Solomon
"I can't think of a better way to help non-profit organizations in the community.

TRANSPORTATION — Greg Toscano
"I think that with so many groups needing so much help, there isn't a better way to do it."

BOOTHS — Walt Glines
"Working at the Garlic Festival is all part of living in Gilroy."

PRINTED PROGRAMS — Chris Filice
"I like the spirit and involvement in the community. I think it is amazing that we can pull it off every year and have it run so smoothly."

Val Filice stirs things up in his "Tank House Ristorante." Filice is lovingly referred to as the Garlic Festival's Godfather. He is credited with making the Festival's Gourmet Alley a success.

The Board of Directors

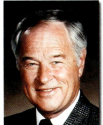

Bob Miller
Vice-President

Barbara Crowther
Secretary

Bert Mantelli
Treasurer

Gene Sakahara
President

Pat Gewin
Director

Lynda Trelut
Director

Anita Trevino
Director

Dr. Eric Nagareda
Director

The year was 1991. It was 3 am on an early July morning. While most Gilroy residents were still fast asleep, Garlic Festival president **Gene Sakahara** had already finished his morning coffee and was busy interviewing with the CBS-TV network.

"Everything goes good with garlic," he told the reporter.

And Sakahara ought to know. He and longtime friend and fellow past president Sam Bozzo created Pacific Rim garlic ginger chicken, which will be a new dish at Gourmet Alley.

Sakahara, who has lived in Gilroy his entire life, believes the Festival represents pride in Gilroy and the community.

"I remember working in the garlic fields when I was young and coming home reeking of garlic. People used to be disgusted by the smell, and it was pretty hard to find a date," Sakahara said. "We have taken the stinking rose and made it prestigious, and that's something to be proud of."

Years before he even imagined being president, Sakahara started his Festival career volunteering for the Presbyterian Church with his children picking up trash. He later went on to run the shuttle buses for the Big Brothers Big Sisters Association, and in 1986 he became the assistant chair of the wine tent.

As his presidency approached, so did the recession of the early '90s. Sakahara feared that he was throwing a huge party and no one would come. Instead, many people chose to take the one-day vacation to Gilroy, and the Festival was a huge success. That same year, Sakahara had the pleasure of signing the $250,000 check to create the ranch side of Christmas Hill Park.

"It was such a thrill!" he said. "Going from being anxious that no one was going to show up to being able to give back so much to the community was a great feeling."

Sakahara also strongly believes the Festival's strength is organization and the teamwork that goes into putting it on.

"I have been to many food Festivals, and I have never seen a group that works so well together like ours," he said.

To keep the Festival successful for years to come, Sakahara said, the Gilroy Garlic Festival Association needs to stay competitive by adding new entertainment attractions and gourmet garlic dishes, as well as keep it family-oriented.

"Our focus is on the family," he said,

Attendance

135,000

What Was New

$3 Million to Non-Profits Since 1979

Office Moved Downtown

Festival Underwrites Purchase of the Ranch Site with City

Queen Appeared on *To Tell the Truth* TV Show
with Kitty Carlisle, David Niven Jr., and Dr. Ruth Westheimer

Volunteer of the Year

Frank Caliri (Gourmet Alley)

Queen Kenda Wilkerson

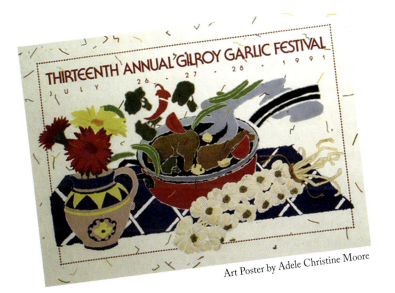

Art Poster by Adele Christine Moore

The Board of Directors

Chris Wheeler
Vice-President

Barbara Crowther
Secretary

Randy Costa
Treasurer

Bob Miller
President

Don Gage
Director

Gordon Kusayanagi
Director

Jeff Martin
Director

Lynda Trelut
Director

Dave Sebald
Director

John Stelling
Director

A year after his reign over the garlic festivities, **Bob Miller** retired from his medical supply company, and he and his wife Mary moved to their Greensboro plantation, where they both sold real estate. Although he is thousands of miles from his former stinky hometown, Miller said he is surprised at how much he is reminded of Gilroy.

"I get amazed every time people here know about the Festival and the 'Garlic Capital of the World,' " Miller said. "I've met quite a few people who have been or plan to make the cross-country trip to the Festival."

Miller attended the first Garlic Festival and said the rise in attendance from a few thousand people in 1979 to 125,409 visitors in 2002 had to do with the heightened popularity of the festivities star—garlic.

"It seems like garlic has become a household word during the past decade, and more and more people are using it," he said.

Miller says peoples' taste buds keep them coming back year after year.

"The entertainment is great, but when you get right down to it, the food is what draws the crowds," he said.

One of Miller's fondest memories of being president was the amount of community involvement. That type of involvement is still prevalent today.

"It's remarkable to see the spirit of the community grow during the months before the Festival," Miller said. "It was always a little sad when the three days of fun were over, but a couple of months later, everyone would be planning again and getting all fired up for the next year."

Miller also said it's heartwarming to see a community come together and put on such a huge event.

"Being president is nice, but the community members make this Festival happen," he said. "As president, you are in charge of seeing things through, but the hard work and determination of the people in the community make this Festival such a success."

As for the future of the celebration of food, entertainment, and the community under the sweltering summer sun, Miller sees that the Festival continues to flourish.

"This makes Gilroy such a great place to live," he said. " … everyone getting together to celebrate and at the same time coming together as a community." 🧄

Attendance
136,000

What Was New

The "DooDoo" Derby

A Combo Plate in Gourmet Alley

Volunteer of the Year

Sandy Stutheit (Gourmet Alley)

Queen Patrisia Garcia

New Combo Plate in Gourmet Alley

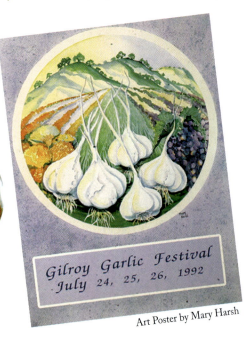
Gilroy Garlic Festival July 24, 25, 26, 1992

Art Poster by Mary Harsh

The Board of Directors

Susan Guardino
Vice-President

Randy Costa
Secretary

Dave Sebald
Treasurer

Chris Wheeler
President

Herb Edde
Director

Alan Ladd
Director

Gregg Giusiana
Director

Jan Froom
Director

Don Gage
Director

Mike Ternasky
Director

Anyone who attended the 1993 Garlic Festival could tell something a little different was going on — the staff was decked out in raspberry-pink polos. **Christine Wheeler,** President, worked with local stores and vendors who sold garlic-affiliated merchandise and made the Festival logo equitable for all.

"We sat down with local vendors and got their opinion on a fair way for both groups to market the logo," she said.

Wheeler, who began her climb to the top in the early '80s, worked her way up from selling strawberry shortcakes to ticket chair to the board of directors and finally vice president and president.

Her year as vice president gave her a chance to learn about all the different aspects of the Festival.

"When you are a chair, you deal with specific responsibilities," she said. "I walked the grounds learning what every-one was doing."

After learning the ropes and finally stepping into the presidential position, Wheeler said she tried to keep one goal in particular in the back of her head. This goal was to stay focused on the path initially set forth by the founding fathers.

"By revisiting your past, you steer your future," she said.

In the fall of 1993, Wheeler attended the International Festival Association Conference in Texas. At the conference, she learned just how highly regarded the Garlic Festival was by other organizations.

"I realized how unique we are in having an almost completely volunteer association," she said. The Festival association only employs three year-round paid staff members.

Along with conferences and special guests, Wheeler said one of the high points of her year as president was traveling to Gilroy's sister city, Takko-Machi, Japan, and learning about the Japanese culture.

"Strive to bring in new events that reflect the Festival's flavor," she said. "As you bring in new people, they bring in fresh perspectives. I've witnessed a lot of creative concepts in recent years."

Wheeler said one of the biggest positives of her presidency is the wonderful friendships she has made.

Attendance
130,0000

What Was New

Children's Area Moved to Creekside of Park

Garlic Festival Cookbook Published

Festival Cooks did Cooking Demonstrations on television, Station KNTV prior to the Festival

Volunteer of the Year

John Blake (Emergency Services)

Queen Jennifer Ross

INTERESTING TIDBIT —

Allergic to Garlic

Coordinator of the Red Cross First Aid Stations at the Festival and 1993 Volunteer of the Year, John Blake, thought he had seen it all over his years of working at the Festival. That was until a gentleman who became seriously ill at the Festival advised him that he was allergic to garlic. After John stabilized him, he directed the visitor to the Gilroy Premium Outlets to shop for the rest of the day — away from the grounds surrounded by the aromas and taste of garlic.

FIFTEENTH ANNUAL

GILROY
GARLIC FESTIVAL

GILROY
GARLIC FESTIVAL
JULY 23, 24, 25, 1993

Art Poster by Joel Quintau

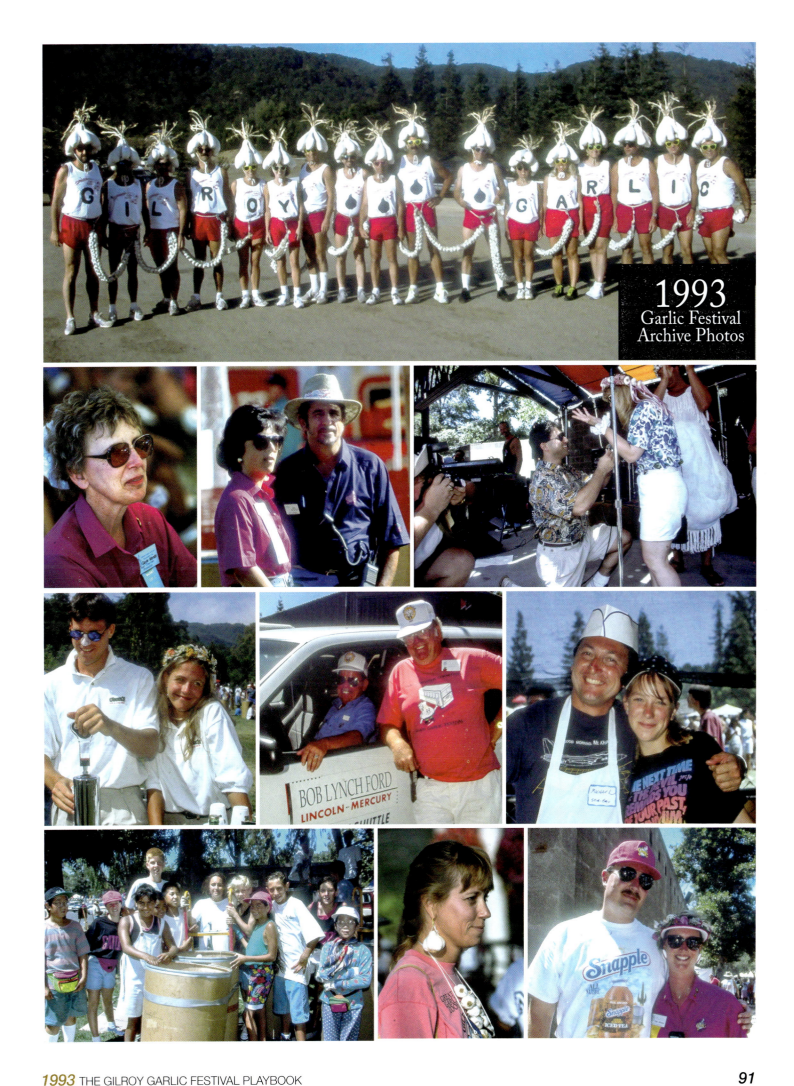

1993
Garlic Festival
Archive Photos

The Board of Directors

Peggy Suyeyasu
Vice-President

Manny Benavidez
Secretary

Erwin Boggs
Treasurer

Lanny Brown
President

Susan Guardino
Past President

Frank Romero
Director

Gregg Giusiana
Director

Leonard Hale
Director

Don Gage
Director

Jeff Speno
Director

Gary Bowe
Director

The year was 1995, and never in his freckled, fair-skinned dreams did Lanny Brown think his year as president would be so scorching hot. With temperatures of 110 degrees on Saturday and 111 degrees on Sunday, it proved to be the warmest in the history of the Festival.

"I'll never forget Dick Nicholls coming up to me with a bent wine glass," Brown said. "For a minute, he had me convinced the heat did it."

Brown, who has also been part of the Gilroy Police Department since 1985, was not only ready to take on the warmth of the Festival, he was prepared to take on the heated challenges brought to the organization in 1995.

The year before Brown's presidency, the Alcohol and Beverage Commission and the Festival's risk-management insurance carrier were looking closely at how operations were run, including how alcohol was served to volunteers.

"In Gourmet Alley, we've got people working with fire and cutting things," Brown said. "We had to make sure things would be safe for everyone."

After working with both groups, Brown and the board of directors changed alcohol regulations to require volunteers working in dangerous areas to be restricted from alcohol consumption during their shifts.

Brown felt people might have thought his role as a police officer had something to do with the change in drinking, but he said he enjoys a good cold one just like anyone else.

The change in alcohol management was minimal. But whenever there is a change, a certain amount of controversy follows.

"The issue was fairly reasonable and made common sense," Brown said. "But it wasn't part of the Festival culture. Whenever there are dynamics changes, you face challenges."

Although the administration had many hurdles to jump, Brown said the dedication and organization of the Garlic Festival Association helped keep things running smoothly, and he was quite pleased with the outcome of the Festival.

"That year went incredibly smooth, and those who did come weren't crowded and packed into the park," he said. "When everything runs smoothly, that's an accomplishment in and of itself."

"We need people not just coming for the weekend and saying 'been there, done that,'" Brown said. "We want people to have such a good time they come again – and bring friends."

Attendance
101,240

What Was New
The Year of the Goofy Hats and 111° Temperature

Construction Phase of Ranch Site Project Began

"Garlic Train" Returned for Saturday and Sunday

Volunteer of the Year –
Jim Murray (Recipe Contest)

Queen Julia Sanchez

GILROY GARLIC FESTIVAL
JULY 28, 29, 30, 1995
Art Poster by Colleen Mitchell-Veyna

Herbie Comes to Life!

Herbie, the official mascot of the children's area, became a real-life character in 1995. He had been delighting kids with his charming newsletter, sent to Garlic Kids Club members annually. Herbie made many appearances throughout the Festival and in the Children's Area. Children were invited to meet him and take a photograph with him.

The Herbie Oath of Honor:
As a member of the Herbie's Garlic Kids Club, I promise to be good, to obey my parents, to be helpful, to share my smile with others at all times, and to eat garlic once a day!

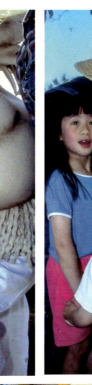

INTERESTING TIDBIT —

It Was a Hot One!!!

The temperatures soared at the 1995 Festival — Saturday clocked in at 110° with Sunday jumping to 111°. Executive Director Dick Nicholls had 1995 President Lanny Brown convinced that the heat had bent one of the commemorative wine glasses …at least for a minute.

1995
Garlic Festival
Archive Photos

The Board of Directors

Ed Mauro
Vice-President

Jeff Martin
Secretary

Kevin Levonius
Treasurer

Peggy Suyeyasu
President

Lanny Brown
Past President

Susan Minyard
Director

Gregg Giusiana
Director

Rose Marie Joyce
Director

Leonard Hale
Director

Don Gage
Director

During **Peggy Burris Suyeyasu**'s 15 years in Gilroy, she taught science at South Valley Junior High School and was involved with the Garlic Festival since its third year.

"I had a friend involved with the association, and it looked like it would be so much fun," Suyeyasu said. "It was a great way to meet some nice people."

Since her time as president, Suyeyasu has been to various festivals and said the Garlic Festival still stands out as far better than any others.

"You can hear good entertainment at many Festivals, but the food here is far superior to any other," she said.

During her time as president, the Festival welcomed its two-millionth visitor at the gate, who was one surprised 6-year-old boy.

"It was extraordinary," Suyeyasu said.

In 1996, the Garlic Festival Association also hit the $4-million mark in money raised for the community of Gilroy.

Suyeyasu said the community that benefits from the funds raised include the people who work the hardest to earn it.

"The best thing about this Festival is it's so fun to volunteer, and it makes people feel like they are involved in something important," she said.

Most presidents run into minor problems, and Suyeyasu had her share. While on stage giving the opening ceremonies speech, the generator died, and she had to welcome everyone through a bullhorn.

"It was inconvenient, but of course, things went on to be wonderful like always," she said.

Another change to the Festival in 1996 was the seeking of public opinion. Suyeyasu and the board created a public forum for Gilroy residents to share their ideas about improving the Festival, which helped the group of Festival committees come up with new strategies to improve the weekend event.

Suyeyasu said the Festival would not be so successful without the capabilities of the workers.

"This organization is a fine-tuned machine," she said. "As president, you don't even know what's going on half the time. Most of the responsibility lies on the committee chairs, and they do a phenomenal job."

Attendance
109,000

What Was New

Rudy Melone Honored on Cook Off Stage
ATM's and Virtual Reality Machine Added
Over 2,000,000 Visitors Since 1979
$4 Million to Non-Profits Since 1979
First Time That the Power Failed

Volunteer of the Year
Shig Nishiguchi (Parking)

Queen Cristin Reichmuth

GILROY GARLIC FESTIVAL JULY 26, 27, 28, 1996
Art Poster by Tom Obata Kobara, Aptos

Remembering Joe Tysdal, Elks Lodge Volunteer

Joe Tysdal was the kind of volunteer everyone wishes they had: Dedicated to the success of each year's Festival, he carried out his volunteer duties to the letter, often with his oxygen tank strapped to his side. Joe had leukemia, but he never let his illness get in the way or asked for preferential treatment. He did whatever was needed to get the job done and keep the Festival going. He and his crew set up Gourmet Alley, and then Joe would work the three days, cooking pasta con pesto and then tearing down the alley. He could not make it to the 1996 Festival and passed away on July 28, 1996, not long after the Festival closed.

The Festival not only gave Suyeyasu friends and a role as president—it gave her love.

"If it weren't for the Garlic Festival, I would have never met my husband," she said.

Suyeyasu, then Peggy Burris, met the 1987 past president Glenn Suyeyasu through working at the Festival. After five years of saying "hello" and making small talk, the presidential couple got married.

"I've always known you can make good friends through this organization, but who would have known I would meet my husband?" she marveled.

Her advice for future success is to continue innovating with new food, new events, and finding other ways of drawing people to the Festival.

After her term as president in 1996, she moved to Napa to care for her mother, who was ill.

Dick Nicholls, CFEE Inducted into Hall of Fame

From the International Festivals & Events Association website:

1993-1994 IFEA (International Festivals & Events Association) Chairman Dick Nicholls, CFEE (Certified Festival & Event Executive), said it was an honor serving IFEA and his IFEA friends as a Director and Officer. He modestly said he could think of others who deserve this honor more than himself, but his record speaks otherwise.

As Executive Director of the Gilroy Garlic Festival, Nicholls has helped the Festival evolve into a world-class event that has been a boon to the town and has poured more than $3 million into community coffers. Exceptional growth has also been part of Nicholls' legacy as IFEA chairman, as he helped the association's membership numbers grow by nearly 100 percent.

Nicholls served on many IFEA committees and was instrumental in helping start the IFEA Foundation. He has successfully initiated a five-year re-marketing plan for his Festival, targeting a more family-oriented audience. The Gilroy Garlic Festival attracts 150,000 in three days, triple the amount of Gilroy residents.

Nicholls said he values the friendships made through IFEA. "I can't express adequately how special these friendships are to me. I feel a special affinity to these people whom I have learned from and been counseled by."

The Organization

IFEA is a 501(c) 6 not-for-profit organization with dedicated, creative, and event-experienced staff ready to help provide the answers, guidance, information, resources, contacts, programming, benefits, and support you need to be successful.

The Certification

Professional Certification (CFEE) enhances professional stature among one's peers; recognizes those who have gone beyond expectations to be the best that they can be; makes a statement to those with whom we do business; provides a leveraged position from which to negotiate and build career success, and sets higher standards for our industry.

The Hall of Fame Award

Known as the association's most prestigious honor, the IFEA Hall of Fame recognizes those outstanding individuals who have made a significant contribution to the Festivals and Events industry and a profound difference in the communities through their exceptional work and achievements they serve, both locally and internationally.

Father of the Festival

FOUNDER & SUPPORTER

Rudy Melone was honored at the Opening Ceremonies of the 1996 Festival.

He had heard the snide remarks. The backhanded jokes. Seen the self-putting-down attitude of the local residents.

But when Rudy Melone sniffed garlic wafting over Gilroy in the heat of summer, he smelled success.

"There was a general air of embarrassment about garlic," said Melone. "An absence of pride. But to me, garlic was everything to be proud about." So he set out to remedy the town's self-esteem.

Appointed as the local Rotary's program chairman, he was looking for something different for a fund-raiser, "...and the aroma of garlic was always there."

Then, Melone, the president of Gavilan College, had heard of Arleux, France, a small town of about 3,000 that annually hosted 80,000 people at its garlic Festival. Arleux was claiming to be the garlic capital of the world.

Well, I thought that was ridiculous," said Melone, who set about researching the matter. "I found out we were the garlic capital of the world."

So he went down to the local coffee shop and talked with the garlic growers who gathered there every morning. "Could we get all the garlic growers together, put on a nice lunch and show the Rotary people the value of garlic!" he asked.

Don Christopher, now one of the largest shippers of garlic products globally, offered his barn. Val Filice, famous for his Italian cooking, lent his recipes and talent. Publicist Caryl Saunders brought in the media, and voila! Says Rudy, "It was a fabulous event."

The following week, Harvey Steinem of the San Francisco Chronicle wrote about it in his column. The bulb was rolling.

Not that there weren't skeptics. Some of the biggest whigs in town laughed aloud at Melone when he suggested a Festival. But he kept asking, and they helped anyway when planning started in early 1979.

In seven months, the first Garlic Festival arrived, bringing hordes of garlic lovers. Because the prudent Festival treasurer, Joe Filice, ordered only 5,000 tickets, no one is really sure how many people were at the first Festival—but everyone agrees it was close to 15,000. "We were selling tickets, collecting them, running back to the ticket booth, and recycling them as fast as we could," laughed Melone. That first Festival netted $19,000.

Now 71 and the president of Saybrook Institute in San Francisco, Melone still keeps his finger on the garlic pulse. He returns each year with his wife, Gloria, 60, to cook their favorites on the Cook-Off stage. He also sits on the strategic planning committee, helping guide the Festival into adulthood.

A lot has changed: 100,000 people regularly come to the Festival each year, and an executive director and staff help run the organization year-round. But a lot has stayed the same: volunteers still staff all committees and governing boards, more than $4 million in profits have been put right back into local organizations, and, perhaps most important: "Garlic is still the star."

"However," says Melone, the stars might never have shone on a small town called Gilroy, whose residents now hold their heads high when recognized as living in "The Garlic Capital of the World."

For that, and for his brilliance, persistence, and years of dedication, this 18th Gilroy Garlic Festival is fondly dedicated to the "Father of the Festival, Rudy Melone."

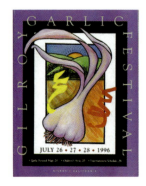

Copy is an excerpt from the 1996 Official Festival Program.

The Board of Directors

Jeff Martin
Vice-President

Patti Hale
Secretary

Jeff Speno
Treasurer

Ed Mauro
President

Peggy Suyeyasu
Past President

Kevin Levonius
Director

Gregg Giusiana
Director

Randy Costa
Director

Sam Bozzo
Director

Don Gage
Director

Rod Pavao
Director

Bruce Williams
Director

Being president of the Garlic Festival was so exciting **Ed Mauro** couldn't stop talking about it, but the media attention that came with it made him speechless.

"It's funny," Mauro said. "The hardest part for me as president was getting in front of the cameras for interviews. It was terrifying."

Talking with reporters and recording a radio commercial in a sound studio was far from the dusty, dirty, sweaty, smelly job he first held at the Festival. Mauro began his Festival career in 1981 by picking up trash. Although it wasn't the most appealing volunteer position, Mauro was happy to be part of it all.

"It was just fun being out there with all the people," he said. "I just wanted to be involved."

Mauro, who used to own Mauro

Stationers in Gilroy, quickly moved up the ladder by getting involved with the beer committee in 1993 through the Chamber of Commerce and moved his way up to the board of directors. His wife, Barbara, also has held a seat on the board.

Stepping into the presidential shoes of the Festival in 1997 brought challenges for Mauro. The previous Festivals of 1995 and 1996 created significant losses in revenue because of a downward spiral in attendance and the constant rise in expenses. Mauro's plate wasn't filled with pesto and scampi but with the problem of keeping the Festival on its feet – and he was up for the challenge.

"I remember the first thing I said to the committee that year was 'put your egos aside,'" he said. "This was going to be a financially challenging year."

Along with the board, Mauro made the decision to bring in Peter Ciccarelli of Peter Ciccarelli and Associates Public Relations. But Mauro didn't want people to get the wrong idea.

"We didn't want the Festival to turn into advertising for big corporations," Mauro said. "We didn't want it to be like 'The Taco Bell Garlic Festival.'"

Before deciding to go the sponsorship route, Mauro spoke with founders Don Christopher and Rudy Melone many times, making sure to keep with the original spirit and goal of the Festival—raising money for the community.

Attendance
122,080

What Was New
Expand & Landscaped Ranch Site
Garlic Kiss Off
Dedicated Festival to Don Christopher
Hired Professional Marketing Firm
Ronald McDonald Visits Children's Area

Volunteers of the Year
Mary Ellen Bena & George Sandoval (Tickets)

Queen Michelle Madrigal

Art Poster by Ben Barnhart, San Martin

Sponsorship turned into marketing and was very subtle. In 1997, Harris Ranch became the official beef of the Festival, and Pepsi became the official soft drink. The companies helped promote the Festival by advertising it on their labels during the months leading up to it.

The Garlic Festival put on promotional events leading up to July along with sponsorship. A few months before the Festival, Mauro and his Vice President Jeff Martin cruised up to Gordon Biersch restaurant in San Jose in tuxes. Escorting actress Darla Hawn of Hollywood, they held the first-ever contest to determine the breath mint of the Festival.

"It was so great," Mauro said. "We had all these guys lined up with different breath mints in their mouths, and after kissing each one, Darla chose the winning mint for the year — Sweet Breath mints."

All of the hard work of the board and the new aggressive publicity paid off — literally. The Festival was back on its feet and brought in roughly $200,000 in sponsorship that year. That year, the Festival gave $201,600 back to the community.

Although Mauro's Festival proved to be a success, he couldn't avoid being anxious about its outcome. Like anyone throwing a party, he worried he would cook the food, provide the entertainment, and no one would show up.

"As president, you have control over what is going on, but once Friday rolls around, you have none," he said.

Of all the great things that come out of the Festival, Mauro believes the camaraderie of 4,000 volunteers makes it so unique.

"One of the highlights of my presidency was being able to walk around and thank as many volunteers as I could for helping out," Mauro said. "They're the ones who make this Festival a success."

Great Garlic Flame at Garlic World off Highway 101, to be placed at the Festival for its twentieth anniversary. Photo: 1998 Randy Costa, Caryl Saunders, Ed Mauro, Rudy Melone, Don and Karen Christopher.

ABOVE: Run for the Stinking Roses — the annual 5K or 10K, was held the Saturday morning of the Festival.

LEFT: Tour de Garlique Bicycle Tour — had more than 1000 riders of all ages tackle the tour courses which varied in length and difficulty but all offered scenic views.

The First Official "Sponsorships" help Festival with Marketing

First Official Beef

First Official Soft Drink

Dedicated to Don

SUPPORT & SPIRIT & INNOVATION

Don Christopher was honored at the Opening Ceremonies of the 1997 Festival.

The long and beneficial relationship between Christopher Ranch and the Gilroy Garlic Festival will be recognized this year when the 1997 Festival is dedicated to Don Christopher.

Over the past 18 years, hard work and dedication by the town of Gilroy have made this unique event the largest and one of the most popular events in the country. Promotion of the Festival by the garlic industry has elevated garlic to the mainstream of American cooking, drawing ever more attention to this unique gathering and the food it showcases. Don Christopher would be the first to acknowledge that the garlic industry has been a primary beneficiary of this tribute to the fragrant bulb.

"An important thing that we learned through our involvement with the Garlic Festival is that promoting garlic and its uses pays off, "says Don. "The Garlic Festival and all of the promotions surrounding it have greatly improved garlic sales."

For Don, the seeds for the Gilroy Garlic Festival were planted in 1978 during a Rotary Club garlic luncheon that he hosted at the ranch. He and Dr. Rudy Melone had invited influential food editors and writers from around the country to taste the fabulous garlic cooking of Gilroy chef Val Filice. Enthusiasm for the food among members of the press and the local business owners was contagious, creating fertile ground for the idea of a town Festival dedicated to garlic.

Rudy, then president of Gavilan College, enlisted support and assistance from the garlic industry and the community. Val Filice was appointed head chef of the Festival's first Gourmet Alley, and other community leaders assumed important roles as committee heads. Still, Rudy and Don's enthusiasm and the financial support from Christopher Ranch launched the first Gilroy Garlic Festival in August of 1979.

Since its inception, the Gilroy Garlic Festival has provided the industry with a beautiful vehicle for promoting garlic. The Fresh Garlic Association, founded in 1978 by Don and other members of the industry, remained in existence until 1992 and was instrumental in promoting the Festival to the national food media and the public.

As California's largest fresh garlic producer, Christopher Ranch grows, packs, and ships almost 60 million pounds of fresh garlic each year. In addition, the company produces many convenient garlic products such as chopped and crushed garlic, whole peeled garlic cloves, pesto sauce, pickled garlic, garlic salsa, garlic barbecue sauce, elephant garlic, garlic braids, and decorative garlic wreaths.

Don continues to be the driving force and constant support for the Gilroy Garlic Festival and has earned gratitude and undying affection for all of his hard work.

Thanks, Don!

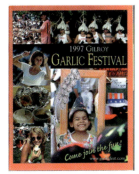

Copy is an excerpt for the
1997 Official Festival Program.

The Board of Directors

Randy Costa
Vice-President

Jim Baggese
Secretary

Jim Habing
Treasurer

Jeff Martin
President

Ed Mauro
Past President

Patty Hale
Director

Jeff Speno
Director

Sam Bozzo
Director

Rod Pavao
Director

Jane Howard
Director

Erwin Boggs
Director

For 1998 president **Jeff Martin**, it was all about sticking to the Festival's mission statement.

"The Gilroy Garlic Festival is established to provide benefits to local worthy charities and non-profit groups by promoting the community of Gilroy through a quality celebration of garlic," it reads, and Martin wanted to make sure this goal was being achieved.

"We had to make sure the Festival was bringing in enough money for the charities and school groups who raise their funds by working at it," he said. "I hate seeing children have to raise their money by selling candy bars door to door."

When making decisions on how to improve revenue for the Festival, Martin worked with fellow past presidents Ed Mauro, Randy Costa, and Jim Habing as a team to try new things business-wise that would eventually have long-term results.

"We all sat down together and looked at the issues at hand," he said. "One of the ways we dealt with it was looking at things and asking ourselves if we would do that in our businesses."

Martin became aware that more promotion was needed during his term as vice president. He and the other team members started asking themselves questions like, "Well, what would Disneyland do?"

"I remember Lynda Trelut saying, 'been there, done that, already bought the hat,' " Martin said. "That was the last thing I wanted people thinking of the Festival."

Before attending his first meeting as president, Martin already had compiled a list of about 50 "what if" possibilities for ways of improving the Festival. One idea was the Garlic Mercantile. The Garlic Festival cookbook sales had been down in the previous years, and the Garlic Festival Association was still selling its merchandise out of a dusty 10-foot-by-10-foot booth. Martin came up with the idea of the Mercantile as sort of a bit of a shopping mall of garlic memorabilia.

"It cut down on a lot of committee work, and it not only streamlined the cookbook, but it also got the other merchandise more visibility," he said. "This way, people may walk in looking for a wine glass and end up leaving with the cookbook, apron, and anything else they needed without looking all over the park for the different booths."

Attendance
130,0000

What Was New

Garlic "McBurgers"

Olympic Style Torch Lights Gourmet Alley

Garlic Merchantile Stores Introduced

Featured the New Garlic Lover's Greatest Hits Cookbook

Volunteer of the Year

Ann Zuhr (Gourmet Alley)

Queen Christina Carrier

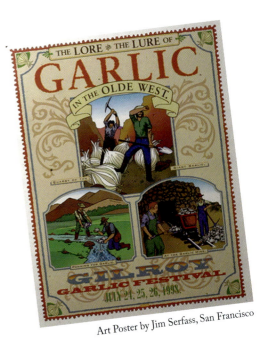
Art Poster by Jim Serfass, San Francisco

Rudy Melone 1925-1998
Beloved Founder of Garlic Festival and Former President of Gavilan College Passes Away

(Remembrance Article, Gilroy Dispatch by Jane Haseldine 12/18/98)

Friends remembered him as a man who embraced life, a true humanitarian, a great communicator and a person who took the ethical high road. He loved the community and would always share a smile or lend an ear. In Gilroy lore, Rudy Melone will be revered as the Father of the Garlic Festival and the Gavilan College President who gave direction to a fledgling institution.

Rudy attended the 20th Anniversary Festival and enjoyed the lighting of the great burning garlic to commemorate the anniversary. The Festival, which began with a lunch, and a core group committed to the idea has poured more than $20 million into the Gilroy community, gained world wide attention and even helped purchase the ranch addition to Christmas Hill Park.

Although Rudy was a Yankee born in Connecticut, he was a true Gilroyan and continued to be active in the community even after he retired to San Francisco 15 years before.

Pictured above with his wife of 28 years, Gloria Melone at the 20th Anniversary Garlic Festival. Gloria and Rudy had three boys, John, Philip, and Michael. At that time, they had four grandsons.

Among other things, Martin remembers a particular volunteer he ran into during his vice-presidential term who gave him an idea to improve Gourmet Alley.

"I remember watching this tired, sweaty guy who was volunteering in Gourmet Alley. He had been working hard the whole week setting the Alley up," he said. "He sat down, and as he took a bite into his pepper steak sandwich, a yellow jacket was sitting on it and bit him in the mouth. I remember hearing him say, 'Man, what is my point doing all of this?'"

Martin, who wanted all volunteers to have a great time, decided to make things more comfortable for the workers. He did away with the rickety old crates that used to form Gourmet Alley and set up a nice airy tent to improve the relentless conditions.

"Those guys would be out there for a week setting that whole thing up and would even find things like dead skunks in the crates when they set it up," Martin said. "Now the tent crew sets it up, and it is a much nicer atmosphere for the workers."

Besides a beehive suddenly appearing on the back of a worker's truck, Martin's Festival ran relatively smoothly. He said the most satisfying feeling ever was closing the gates on Sunday and relaxing with his friends.

"It was the best feeling in the world," Martin said. "All my friends were there, and we were all tired, dirty, smelly but also really happy."

"The Garlic Festival was his baby and it was amazing that he was in San Francisco and never was out of touch with one thing. If we didn't see him for a year he still knew exactly what was going on like a proud parent. He was always right there. His council whenever we had a problem was invaluable."

Jeff Martin, 1998 President

"It is a huge loss for me personally and a tremendous loss for the community. He understood the Festival could never be the same as the first one and that it would grow and evolve and become a living dynamic instead of a snapshot. He was an extremely ethical person and always chose the high road. It is wonderful to see what he brought to this community in 20 years. We will go on, but his leadership will always be with us."

**Richard Nicholls
Executive Director**

Founder Rudy Melone at his last Festival.

Garlic Mercantile Opens

Eleven smaller booths that were scattered throughout the grounds of the Festival were combined into two 1,200 square-foot retail spaces, one located on the Ranch side and one near the Amphitheater on the park side. The concept was simple: to combine all the Festival souvenirs, cookbooks, wine glasses, and posters into a space where customers could wander among garlic-mania displays while searching for that perfect gift or memento commemorating their visit to the 20th Annual Gilroy Garlic Festival.

Offerings and an updated line of collectibles were added. Some items added in 1998 included a few more titles of recipe books, art posters (including the latest winner), and a lot more garlicky items.

Val Filice Recognized for His Contributions to the Festival

Known as the Godfather of the Festival, Val Filice and Gourmet Alley were the cornerstones of the Festival. From the first Festival, Val lent his cooking expertise, helping make the Festival THE best food Festival in the nation.

Co-founders, Rudy Melone and Don Christopher were on hand, along with then Mayor Mike Gilroy to congratulate Val at the opening ceremonies.

1998 Garlic Festival MAP

Gate 4

Rain Room

Gavilan Kennel Club

Gate 1
To main parking lot

Amphitheater Stage

Garlic Festival Map Legend

- Wine Tent
- Program & Ticket Booth
- Garlic Topping & Braiding
- Shade Tent
- Garlic Mercantile
- Rest room
  *Handicap restrooms are located in all restroom areas except the children's area
- Booths
- Information/keeper
- Beer Tent
- Micro Brew Tent

2000
Garlic Festival
Archive Photos

Ri
Vic

J i
th
w
world

Ha
comm
electr
impo

"V
Festiv

Se
his sh
meet
and n

"I
the p

He
was

Vo
pins
Festiv

Atte
100,4

Who

Shad

Garlic

Year

Supe
and S

Volu

Isaac
Sabra

Que

122   124   THE GILROY GARLIC FESTIVAL PLAYBOOK *2000*

The Board of Directors

Kurt Chacon
Vice-President

Steve Ynzunza
Secretary

Janie Mardesich
Treasurer

Ric Heinzen
President

Jim Habing
Past President

Barbara Mauro
Director

Gena Sakahara
Director

George Minerva
Director

John Locey
Director

Ric Heinzen was an engineer and owner of ACS, a Gilroy firm making electrical controls in 2001. He gave out pocket protectors to all the other Festival officials to help build camaraderie. If he caught them without the pocket protector, he'd tell them they were "out of uniform" and not playing their nerdy roles.

"We didn't have slide rules, but everyone was given a pocket protector with a pen and screwdriver," he said.

But Heinzen wasn't always taking on the nerd role as an engineer; he once was just another boy growing up around the stinky herb that makes Gilroy famous.

"My mother wanted her boys to work in the summer; we moved to Gilroy in 1962," Heinzen remembered. "On Fifth Street and Miller, all there was were old prune trees and garlic fields. She took us during the summer months, and we topped garlic and worked in the fields. It was part of our summer routine for three summers before I turned 16 and could get a real job."

Heinzen learned some valuable skills working in the garlic fields, and the poster for the 2000 Garlic Festival reminded him of those days.

"We were working for Joseph Gubser garlic, the original garlic king before Christopher Ranch. I hoed garlic fields, and when the committee selected the poster, it had a bucket of garlic with the Gavilan Hills in the background," he said. "It brought me back to my youth. I still use it as a greeting card today. Yeah, it made it special for me."

Heinzen never forgot those days, and in Gubser's honor, he brought his old boss' widowed wife with him to the 2001 Festival as a guest of honor.

"I always respected her husband," he said. "He was a good businessman."

But the engineer also had to be quick on his feet and make some tough decisions during his year running the show.

On opening day, he noticed that the beef used for the famous pepper steak sandwiches—a beloved traditional dish of the alley—smelled "funny," Heinzen said.

"When Gourmet Alley opened, it became an issue because, from their point of view, it was bad meat," Heinzen remembers. "To be ready to open and find out you have 17,000 or 18,000 pounds of meat you can't serve, it's a stressful situation."

Attendance
101,870

What Was New
Weather Vanes Big Seller in Merchantile

Local Cook-Off King Adam Sanchez

Got Milk Extreme Skateboarding Exhibition

Volunteers of the Year
Erwin Boggs (Retail)

Nancy Fohner (Tickets)

Queen Linsay Michele Smith

Gilroy Garlic Festival
July 27, 28, & 29, 2001
Art Poster by Kris Knutson, Photographer, Gilroy

A butcher volunteer said the meat was still good and not a safety hazard, but Heinzen was concerned about how the situation might damage the Festival's reputation.

"It's the perception that people will have that it's not good," he said.

Heinzen and other volunteers raced to local supermarkets and bought as much beef as possible to replace the meat for Friday's crowds. We received more meet from the Bay Area for the remaining two days. The integrity of the Garlic Festival was not only preserved; it was enhanced.

Bookending the Festival with another stressful situation, on Sunday night, Heinzen looked up to see a helicopter with a searchlight circling the park as the Festival came to a close. He soon learned a man and his girlfriend had had a fight in the Vineyard Stage area, and the man tried to run her over with his car.

But despite these incidents, Heinzen said the Festival went off reasonably smoothly, and guests and volunteers enjoyed themselves.

The big seller in the merchandise booths was large weather vanes, and people lined up for hours to buy them. And the milk industry's "Got Milk?" extreme skateboard exhibition drew large crowds throughout the three days.

"It is when everyone comes together to have a good time," he said. "Everyone gets a satisfying feeling; knowing what you and others have worked on over the past six to eight months of planning."

Heinzen received some criticism for raising the prices of the dishes in Gourmet Alley, but he stressed this action was necessary to make the culinary heart of the Festival profitable. He had looked at the cost of ingredients for Gourmet Alley dishes on a computer program that Sysco, a food supplier, had, and he decided changes were necessary.

"The Festival is a business, and people have to consider that aspect of it," he said. "I learned that the Festival has its own momentum. The changes are best in small steps. You have to make changes over a period of two to three years. It needs to be fun and benefit the community.

But the board of directors needs to look at it analytically and see if it meets our mission statement."

"… The focus of the food Festival has to be on food," he said. "Gourmet Alley is our signature of the Festival. People come for the food. Without Gourmet Alley, we'd look a lot like other Festivals. 🧄

The Board of Directors

Janie Mardesich
Vice-President

Don Kludt
Secretary

Barbara Mauro
Treasurer

Kurt Chacon
President

Ric Heinzen
Past President

Gena Sakahara
Director

John Zekanoski
Director

Jim Baggese
Director

Jennifer Speno
Director

John Locey
Director

When **Kurt Chacon** moved to Gilroy from San Jose in 1988, he didn't know a soul in town. He just wanted a quieter lifestyle for his young family.

"That year, I poured beer for the Chamber of Commerce," Chacon said.

"Transportation, assistant to utilities … the next thing you know, you're spending all your time at the Garlic Festival."

And then, suddenly, Chacon found himself named Festival president for 2002.

It was something that Chacon probably never would've done in any other community.

"Absolutely not! Part of the problem is that it's not as easily accessible as the Garlic Festival," Chacon said about being involved in a major community event. "I think (the Festival) is a fast track to being a part of the community,"

Chacon did not want to mess too much with the Festival's successful recipe,

he only made a few minor changes, but they made for positive results.

"I relocated half of the art vendors to the park side," he said. "Trying to look down the road a little ways, I thought it would create flow to the park side. It created a draw into the south. It also allowed the two large shade tents on the ranch site."

Chacon also opened up more parking for Festival guests by grading fields and providing foot access. Parking is always a big concern for presidents, he said.

Volunteering for the Festival is a good way for newcomers to the area to make friends and become part of the Gilroy community. Chacon said he knows this from personal experience.

"It's very self-rewarding. You feel good about being part of something," he said.

"I would love to have more of the new residents get involved somehow. When you move into a small, close-knit town, you tend to feel like an outsider.

Getting involved in the Garlic Festival is one way to get involved in the mainstream."

And the Festival helps foster camaraderie among the citizens, he believes.

"I think the Garlic Festival and how it's getting everyone involved is what's great about the community of Gilroy," he said. "It allows people to go out and work beside someone and make friends with people you wouldn't generally get involved with."

Attendance
125,405

What Was New
Divided Arts & Crafts (Park & Ranch)

"Faces in the Crowd"

Herbie Bobble Head Dolls in Merchantile

Volunteers of the Year
Brian Jones (Garlic Grove)

Mary Yates (Signs)

Ted Kubota (Tickets)

Queen Vanessa LaCorte

HERBIE MAKES HIS DEBUT AT THE TWENTY-FOURTH FESTIVAL!

Gilroy Garlic Festival
July 26, 27, & 28, 2002

Art Poster by Ruth Johnson Irving, Gilroy

2002

2007

Miss Gilroy Garlic follows in Mother's Footsteps

"I've wanted to be the Garlic Queen ever since I can remember," said Vanessa LaCorte (18), who had lived in Gilroy all of her life. "I've always looked forward to the Festival and all of the excitement that surrounds it."

For LaCorte, a person who likes to be in the middle of things, being Miss Gilroy Garlic 2002 came naturally.

"I wouldn't describe myself as shy," LaCorte said. "I've always liked to be around people and be involved in whatever is going on. Being the Garlic Queen is so fun because I got to be involved in everything, met new people, and gave back to the community."

LaCorte had recently graduated from Notre Dame High School in Salinas, where she had partici- pated in volleyball and softball. She was to attend col- lege at St. Mary's of Moraga near San Francisco in the fall as a pre- law major.

Displaying her versatility during the Miss Gilroy Garlic Pageant, LaCorte also won the Miss Congeniality Award, speech com- petition, and earned a scholarship from Bob Lynch Ford.

"This is just a great opportunity to be a role model for the town," LaCorte said. "I know when I was little, I looked up to the queens, and I'm looking forward to that. I've already learned a lot of leadership skills, which has helped my communication—it has made me even more outgoing."

Taking a quick look at LaCorte's family tree, it is no surprise how she grew from a little girl with a dream into a queen.

LaCorte's mother, Karen LaCorte, is a former Bonanza Days Queen—the city's annual celebration that preceded the Gilroy Garlic Festival. Her father, Frank LaCorte, is a former relief pitcher for the Houston Astros. LaCorte is also related to 2002 Ms. San Benito Rodeo Natalie LaCorte and 2002 Hollister Independence Rally cover girl Eden Gonzales.

Vanessa graduated from St Mary's Moraga. She was a pharmaceutical rep before marrying Casey Courneen. They will be married nine years in August and have three beautiful children, Fiona, Sloane, and Axel. Along with her love of fashion, Vanessa is interested in nutrition and fitness and enjoys cooking and baking.

ABOVE: Vanessa LaCorte, 2002 Miss Gilroy Garlic and **INSET**: Sig Sanchez with Vanessa's mother, Karen LaCorte in 1976 when she was crowned Miss Gilroy as part of the Bonanza Days Celebration.

Home of the Gilroy Garlic Festival

25th Anniversary Kick-off

The Gilroy Garlic Festival celebrated the start of its 25th season at Bonfante Gardens Family Theme Park on the Saturday of the same weekend the park closed its gates for the season.

Mayor Tom Springer gave a note-worthy nod to the Festival's founder, the late Rudy Melone, during the proclamation ceremony kicking off of "Garlic Day." Val Filice, the Festival's co-founder and Gourmet Alley master chef, announced during a cooking demonstration that jars of his pasta sauce would soon be hitting the supermarkets.

Filice said he was working on a pasta sauce product called "Garlic Godfather." The recipe would be the same pasta sauce cooked at the Festival, and the label would include a picture of Filice on it.

Don Christopher, Val Filice and John Locey talk to KSBW/Action News Sunrise anchor, Kate Callaghan at Gilroy Gardens.

A Celebration of Garlic – and Gilroy Goodness

(Kira Hagenbuch Monica, the daughter of former and longtime Dispatch columnist Huck Hagenbuch wrote this tribute to the Festival spirit. October 17, 2002)

Some people have well-loved Christmas traditions or annual summer vacations. I, on the other hand, have the Garlic Festival. I've attended every year since I was 12—I haven't missed one. This was not a goal I set; it just sort of happened. At first, I thought it was certainly not something to brag about; a pretty embarrassing statistic. But lately—as I've begun to feel somewhat like the Cal Ripken of the Garlic Festival—I've grown rather proud of the fact. It's special because there aren't many people that have a Gilroy.

The friendships, support, and sense of community are inspiring. They exist day in and day out—the Festival is simply the time of year when the rest of the world gets to see them. Through the Festival, people have come to know my hometown. And the Garlic Capital leaves a lasting impression.

My sister and I checked out the first Festival with my parents in 1979. I remember relaxing beneath expansive trees, savoring my first pepper steak sandwich. I was hooked from that moment. Within a few years, I was stamping hands at Christmas Hill and serving garlic bread in the Gilroy High Girls Basketball booth. It was a great way to earn money for the church or school groups. But just as importantly, the Festival was the halfway point, an event that brought classmates and friends together for a midsummer catch-up session. You could see who was still dating, who'd broken up, and who was having a summer fling.

Each summer had its drama, its own story. Guys without shirts donned cutoff shorts and spray bottles. Girls shrieked during catfights. The Festival was quite the social scene. In our minds, we were gracious hosts and thrilled to be inviting thousands of strangers into our backyard.

By college, the Festival took on a new dimension. It was an event that reunited us Gilroy High grads and gave us the opportunity to acquaint our college friends with the Festival. After letting them in on how to sneak in on various back roads and where to park off Miller Avenue, we'd make our way to Gourmet Alley, talking about Gilroy and pointing out ex-boyfriends. But the college friends didn't have much interest in the trip down memory lane; they simply wanted to eat, listen to some music, and then get out of the sun. Although they didn't seem to have the full appreciation for our Festival, at least it was another group turned on to the delights of pasta con pesto and calamari.

As my fellow Gilroyans and I entered the working world, our lives became more detached. But year after year, the Garlic Festival was our common ground. Although many of us relocated—including a move to Seattle for me—we enjoyed bumping into each other, in a food line, or at the amphitheater. Sometimes I'd return with a Seattleites in tow (I'm bringing three this year). The North Westerners relished the sunshine, good food, and the opportunity to explore the Golden State. And those that haven't made the trip yet still look forward to this time of year—they hover around my cubicle, waiting for me to return with a giant bag of Garlic Kettle Corn and stories of overindulgence.

The Festival is a celebration of delicious food and community spirit. It's become a ritual for many that didn't even grow up in Gilroy. For those of us that did, it's a time to be proud. The entire town works together to pull off an extraordinary party—and for me, it always feels like it's saying "welcome home." I'm thankful that the tradition continues and that I have my midsummer getaway to look forward to each year. Though I may not be buttering up the bread, I still hit the girl's basketball booth every year and tell friends, "This is MY booth. I worked here …" and it makes me smile—grateful for the memories I have and the ones yet to be created.

The Board of Directors

John Zekanoski
Vice-President

Don Kludt
Secretary

Jodi Heinzen
Treasurer

Janie Mardesich
President

Kurt Chacon
Past President

Gregg Giusiana
Director

Dave Sebald
Director

Jim Baggese
Director

Jennifer Speno
Director

Judy Lazarus
Director

During the 2003 Garlic Festival, **Janie Mardesich** had as much responsibility as anyone involved with Gilroy's world-famous event.

It was her year as Festival president, and she was determined to have as much fun as anyone there. For Mardesich, having fun at the Garlic Festival is not a volunteer's privilege. It is their duty.

"If we have a good time, I guarantee our guests will have a good time. I really believe that," Mardesich said.

Her baseball jersey selection for the official 2003 shirt reflects that sense of fun and teamwork.

Mardesich, a 28-year Gilroy resident at the time, had some favorite ways to have a good time at the Festival. She'd catch the Corvairs and ShaBoom performances and always stop by the Cook-Off stage. But more than anything, Mardesich would always try to "find humor in the hiccups," the things that invariably didn't go exactly as planned.

"Things run pretty smoothly until the week of the event when everything gets set up and put in place," Mardesich said, recalling incidents such as a vendor who placed its booth in another vendor's spot.

Mardesich was in her 17th year as a Garlic Festival volunteer, an annual act of giving back to the community that she saw as a sort of a second career. Her Garlic Festival career started when she helped her husband Dave work the parking lot for a service club.

"I loved it. Everyone was in the same boat – mud and dirt," Mardesich said, referring to the unpaved lot where the parking attendants worked. I enjoyed watching the people come and go, and seeing how happy they were to be at the Festival was terrific."

After her parking lot stint, Mardesich moved on to surveying guests for three years—to find out where people came from, what they liked, and what they'd like to see done differently.

"I kept having fun, so I kept getting more involved," Mardesich said.

The mother of two became co-chair and later chairman of the Children's Area, a place she called "a Festival within a Festival."

No matter what her role with the Garlic Festival was, the last full weekend in July has been a Mardesich family holiday.

"Nothing gets in the way of the Festival weekend," Mardesich said.

Attendance
132,751

What Was New
All Star Team Wore Jerseys

Garlic Festival Day at SF Giants Game

Herbie in a Tux

Ginger, Garlic, Chicken Stir Fry (SakaBozzo)

Volunteers of the Year –
Janie Leibich (Recipe Contest)

Mike McCarthy (Utilities)

Queen Melissa Noto

HERBIE PUT ON A TUX TO CELEBRATE THE FESTIVAL'S TWENTY-FIFTH ANNIVERSARY.

Art Poster by Jim Serfass, San Francisco

2003
Garlic Festival
Archive Photos

Photo of Karri Duke and group at their first appearance at the Gilroy Garlic Festival in 1979.

"Gilroy Garlic Festival's Little Package of Dynamite"

A Nickname Given To Karri Duke By The Belly Dancing Community

Karri Duke belly danced her way into the hearts of many a Festival goer during her over 25 years of performances at the Festival. From that first day in 1979 to her last appearance in 2003, she and her fellow dancers never disappointed. In 2003, Duke was the sole member of an exclusive club—having performed at every Festival since 1979.

At the very first Festival, the dancers were Duke, her twin sister, Emily, a performer who went by the stage name of Una and two others. In her final year, about three-dozen dancers performed for the crowd, including several men and children.

Karri remembers her years performing at the Festival fondly. One fun memory was arriving at the Festival in a friend's tour bus, making arriving so easy with her troupe. Once on the grounds, however, they had to work their way through the crowd of thousands. A biker group spread out and made a path for her and her troupe, escorting them across the park to the stage where they were to perform.

In another reminiscence, she notes that she feels the success of performing for 25 years at the Festival was because she would bring the best belly dancer performers from all over California to share the stage with her every year. She noted that her Gilroy Parks & Recreation studio dancers, the Soroya Dance Company, appreciated having a shorter time on stage, especially for the years that experienced record-breaking heat. "My troupe and I gained so much experience and recognition through numerous festivals throughout California due to the reputation of the Gilroy Garlic Festival."

In addition to festival gigs, Karri acknowledges that the Garlic Festival appearances led to many other gigs, parties, and performances and gained her a job performing for "Dancers Ala Carte" as one of their house dancers.

Duke has received several awards over the years, including being named 1991 Ms. America of Belly Dance in

San Francisco. And in 1993, she took first place in the Miss Santa Clara County Muscle Classic. "Belly dancing keeps me young," she noted in a Gilroy Dispatch article written in 2003.

Karri and her husband, Mike, moved to Cleburne, Texas, shortly after her 25th appearance at the Festival. She considers being the only performer who performed from 1979 to 2003 her most significant honor.

The Board of Directors

Jennifer Speno
Vice-President

Micki Pirozzoili
Secretary

Jodi Heinzen
Treasurer

John Zekanoski
President

Janie Mardesich
Past President

Gregg Giusiana
Director

Hugh Davis
Director

Jim Baggese
Director

Steve Welch
Director

At the onset of his presidency, **John Zekanoski** set out to complete several goals. One of them was to make the famous flaming garlic bulb a Bay Area icon. To do this, he hauled the giant herb from location to location in the back of his pick-up truck whenever there was a photo opportunity. Zekanoski's wife would come home to find the enormous bulb sitting in the driveway in the evenings. She would just shake her head.

"So I lived with this bulb for a week," he said. "I'd be driving down (U.S.) 101 with the bulb in the back of my truck, and everyone would be honking and cheering."

Anyone who knows Zekanoski agrees that living with the giant garlic was more of a presidential perk for him than anything else. They would also tell you his lighthearted humor and good nature allows him to find fun in any situation and that his energy is infectious.

"He's awesome. Absolutely the best,"

said Mike Smith, who worked on the advisory committee. "He's a great leader, and he tells some pretty good jokes too."

After a year of arduous preparation, Zekanoski, like every other preceding president, had but three days of festivities to witness the fruits of his labor before passing the torch to next year's leader.

He started early Sunday by having breakfast with representatives from Takko-Machi, one of Gilroy's five sister cities. Then he made his way to the Festival site for some more meet and greet with volunteers and guests.

Most of Zekanoski's presidential duties involved planning activities and coordinating committees months before the pyro chefs in Gourmet Alley lit their first flames. So when the Festival finally arrived, Zekanoski got to play the part of "head cheerleader." His main job was to root everyone on as they cooked the food and served guests.

"When people feel good about themselves, they do well at their job," he said. "And that's my job."

Zekanoski would typically be found playfully razzing volunteer workers or talking with vendors during the Festival. And after the guests went home, the Festival was his playground.

Zekanoski strapped on his roller blades to test out the Got Milk Gravity Tour ramp on Saturday evening, then skated around the empty booths.

Zekanoski moved from New England to Gilroy 18 years ago and has attended 17 consecutive Garlic Festivals. He started as a volunteer on the utilities committee. 🧄

Attendance
122,675

What Was New
Attendance Reached 3 Million

Garlic Fried Baloney Sandwich
(By SakaBozzo)

Second Combo Plate Added
(Gourmet Alley)

Volunteer of the Year
Tom West (Communications)

Queen Alika Spencer

HERBIE IS READY FOR WORK AS A PYRO CHEF IN GOURMET ALLEY.

Art Poster by Karen Hinds, Brentwood

2004
Garlic Festival
Archive Photos

The Board of Directors

Micki Pirozzoli
Vice-President

Judy Lazarus
Secretary

Steve Welch
Treasurer

Jennifer Speno
President

John Zekanoski
Past President

Hugh Davis
Director

Dave Sebald
Director

Kirsten Carr
Director

Jeff Martin
Director

A day in the life of the Garlic Festival's president is never still. That's one thing that **Jennifer Speno**, the event's 2005 president, learned over the weekend as she circled the Festival grounds, moving from chairperson to chairperson as she coordinated the Festival's 27 separate committees.

"We've had problems, but they're great problems to have," Speno said, referring to long lines and ticket shortages that occurred Saturday.

The petite mom of two and former Garlic Festival queen was an unstoppable blur, darting to help with ticket recycling, free water stations, and other on-demand tasks during the busy weekend. Still, the actual stress for Speno began last year, she said, when she realized that the entire Festival, run by John Zekanoski in 2004, would soon be her responsibility. The stress level hasn't dropped, according to past president Jeff Martin.

"If I know Jennifer, the stress level went up then, and it won't come down until this is all over," Martin said, sweeping his hand across the crowd.

The Festival's run had been positive Friday and Saturday, but Speno wouldn't let herself get too excited on Sunday. She had a feeling something stressful— perhaps a repeat of Saturday's rush— would happen.

At 2:30 pm, it did. Festival gate number one, situated in an area cut off from communications by dodgy radio and cell phone reception was running low on child/ senior tickets. Speno, unable to reach anyone by radio, took off for the gate's stand to assess the situation in person. Ducking onto back roads that skirted vending stations and dodging between refuse bins and volunteers as she sped across the length of the Festival grounds, she reached the gate in time to begin recycling tickets, directing volunteers, and calling on help from Festival directors scattered throughout the park.

"Once Friday comes, the Festival takes on a life of its own," Speno said. "Our job is to make sure committees work together, but our real work is the decisions and meetings through the year."

One of Speno's more challenging decisions centered on the Festival's transportation costs. In 2004, the group spent more than $65,000 on transit, shuttling

Attendance
129,644

What Was New
Demonstration Stage (Sponsored by Calphalon)
Garlic Queen Becomes President (First)

Volunteer of the Year
Mike Zukowski (Parking)

Appreciation of Service Award
Majid Bahriny

Queen Aisha Zaza

HERBIE ENTERS THE COOKING CONTEST ON THE COOK-OFF STAGE.

GILROY GARLIC FESTIVAL
July 29, 30, & 31, 2005

Art Poster by Jennifer Lau, New York

attendants to and from the grounds, and the board was looking for ways to cut costs in 2005.

"One way to save was to go without air conditioning on the buses, but we decided to spend a little more to keep people happy," Speno said. "We wanted to keep costs down, but we also wanted to balance what was necessary and what was going to benefit our community."

The same thought guided Speno and the rest of the committee when the Milk Advisory Board pulled funding for their "Got Milk?" concert stage just months before the event.

Instead of dipping into volunteer proceeds to pay performers, they made the stage into a karaoke stage and found a sleeper of a hit. The tent was packed with spectators before noon.

"I think one of our biggest challenges will be after the Festival," Speno said. "We have the loss of (longtime executive director) Dick Nicholls this year, and we're looking at getting a new executive director by January. That person will have to get

acquainted with our seasoned staff and the community that drives this Festival."

The work of a past president is never done, according to Festival past president John Zekanoski, but work on the committee can wait after the Festival's final cleanup is done Wednesday. Right now, Speno's mind is on a long-overdue vacation.

"Every year, a few of us from the Festival go to Lake Shasta to go house boating," Speno said. "The biggest decision we make when we go is which drink to have next." ⚜

Dollars raised for local charities since 1979:

$6,918,105

The Gilroy Garlic Festival thanks you!

2005
Garlic Festival
Archive Photos

Richard "Dick" Nicholls 1944-2005

Garlic One

Fondly Remembered by Family, Friends and the Community

(Remembrance Article, Gilroy Dispatch by Lori Stuenkel, June 2005)

When it came to Festival planning, **Dick Nicholls** did not leave anything to chance, said Joann Kessler, the Festival's assistant director who worked with Nicholls for 15 years.

"He followed through on pretty much everything, and he was just really good at his job," she said. "He knows so much about the Festival, things that no one else knows. He would know from day to day what to expect, especially on the grounds: where there's going to be a lot of traffic, and when there's going to be a lot of people in line for the shuttle bus, and he was anywhere he needed to be."

A parade of volunteer Festival presidents who worked with Nicholls through the years echoed the sentiment and shared a fondness for the man who loved to meet for lunch to talk about family or recent investments.

"He made the job very easy. He stood behind me the entire time—stood beside me the entire time. He kept track of the details and didn't let anything fall through the cracks," said John Zekanoski, president of the 2004 Festival.

Zekanoski said Nicholls had an easy and graceful style that allowed him to consider the needs of the entire Festival community in decision-making. That community includes roughly 4,000 volunteers who show up each year to serve up garlicky pesto, mix smoothies or direct traffic.

When asked about his favorite part of the Festival or whether one year made an impression, Nicholls would shrug off the question and say that it all stood out to him.

After growing up in Morgan Hill, Nicholls lived in Gilroy until he moved to Salinas several years ago. He first volunteered at the inaugural Festival in 1979, parking cars. He was hired as executive director for the sixth Festival in 1985.

During his tenure, the Festival raised about $6.5 million for local charities and community groups and put Gilroy on the map as "Garlic Capital of the World."

"He has been the Festival," Police Chief Gregg Giusiana said. "He's been the one person that's been there through it all. He's going to be very sorely missed. He was sort of the rock there."

Nicholls was diagnosed with cancer March 21. At the time, he said he planned to continue working as much as possible while undergoing treatment. He followed through, Kessler said.

"If he was not going to treatment or had a doctor's appointment, he was in this office," she said. "Even after chemotherapy, he would work 9 to 5. Up until the last month, he has been here more than not."

He was admitted to Salinas Memorial Hospital last Friday, and died there Wednesday afternoon at the age of 60. He is survived by his wife, Brigitte, and 20-year-old twin sons Justin and Jerrod, who just graduated from Hartnell College.

Nicholls always had time for those who would stop by his downtown office, regardless of the stresses or strains of the day, said Sam Bozzo, a past president and part the goofy Saka-Bozzo cooking team, with Gene Sakahara.

He recalled a dinner at a down-home crab restaurant when Nicholls stooped to the level of the off-the-wall team amidst the atmosphere of paper-covered tables piled high with crab legs.

"Gene and I were kind of acting up" Bozzo said, "and I remember there was this loaf of bread that just sailed across the table. It was just so out of character for Dick."

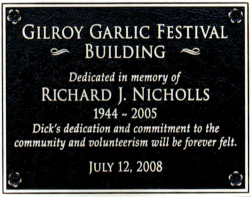

In 2008, the Festival moved to new building located at 7600 Monterey Street. The building was dedicated to Richard J. Nicholls in his memory.

ABOVE: His two boys, Justin and Jerrod with their mother, Brigitte Nicholls at the dedication ceremony.

"Though successful in the early years, we were dangerously close to being a big beer bust in 1986 when Dick was hired as Executive Director. Dick believed that to keep the Festival community oriented, we needed to focus on the volunteers… and the food.

"His ability to direct our growth through an ever-changing path of volunteers was remarkable. He was a master of developing consensus.

"He joined the International Festival and Events Association as an observer, to learn from other venues. Over time he turned the tables on them. As we grew, they were coming to us for advice. That was because of Dick Nicholls."

John Locey, President
1986 Garlic Festival Association

"Dick walked his talk. He was an exemplary father and role model for his sons Jerrod and Justin. His vision and foresight implemented a transition from just fun in the sun for the young to a premier food Festival and family activity.

"On Sundays, he used to gauge our success by looking out at the park and observing the number of strollers."

Gene Sakahara, President
1991 Garlic Festival Association

Gloria Melone, the widow of co-Garlic Festival founder Rudy, said she admired Nicholls for his ability to work with the different chairs of numerous Festivals, and the 4,000 ground-level volunteers who help run the three-day event.

"There are thousands of volunteers in the Garlic Festival and it takes a special kind of person and character and personality to be able to bring together these people, where they can willingly volunteer hours of hardship, time and money and effort—and to get them to move together smoothly," Melone said.

In his career, Nicholls, received accolades from his peers, most notably being inducted into the International Festivals and Events Association's Hall of Fame in 1996. The association's members nominated him for making significant contributions to the Festival and events industry. Nicholls also was one of the founders of CalFest, the California and Nevada Festivals and Events Association, and a past board member.

When Sakahara was president in 1991,

he was No. 2 on Nicholls' speed-dial.

"When I was past president, I asked 'Am I still speed dial No. 2?' He said, 'Of course, you're my No. 2'," Sakahara said. "As time would go on, he would say, 'Uh, uh, you've dropped to No. 29.'"

"He was very good at working through issues and taking a very calm view of things," said Giusiana, also a past president.

Some wondered on the Wednesday of Festival week, just what tricks Nicholls had up his sleeve—that were unknown even to seasoned veterans of the Festival.

"What don't we know that he used to take care of?" Zekanoski said. "He did so much of the little things. … Who did he call that we don't know he called?"

The Festival's board members have already dedicated themselves to making this year's Festival on July 29, 30 and 31 as successful as if Nicholls were attending.

"For his sake, we need to make sure that nothing falls through the cracks," Kessler said.

"…The Festival's imprint has stamped the very soul of Gilroy. Its mark is left in volunteerism, in generosity, in working to-gether for common goals, in teaching young people to be a part of their community and in showing the world in fabulous fashion, why Gilroy is great.

"Therein lies the spirit of Dick Nicholls, who carefully helped weave the beautiful tapestry that is our hometown. Dick Nicholls' ego always rode in the back seat. The Festival, and its volunteers came first…"

Gilroy Dispatch, June 24, 2005

The Board of Directors

Judy Lazarus
Vice-President

George Minerva
Secretary

Ed Struzik
Treasurer

Micki Pirozzoli
President

Jennifer Speno
Past President

Steve Welch
Director

Garry Offenberg
Director

Roy Shackel
Director

Jeff Martin
Director

President, **Micki Pirozzoli** might be small in stature, but she had a nickname, "The Puff of Dust," which she had earned. During the 2006 Festival, she was everywhere, checking on things, looking ahead, and providing leadership and concern. Pirozzoli's enthusiasm and warm personality – and spark-plug energy – made her a well-liked president.

The 2006 Garlic Festival had a number of firsts:

1) Executive Director Brian Bowe brought new energy and technical skills to the Festival.

2) A new accounting system to count tickets was installed.

3) Guests could purchase e-tickets online. Over 2,000 tickets were purchased online that first year.

The Garlic Idol contest debuted. It began with weeks of radio tryouts that culminated with stage performances on the Festival's first day. On Sunday, the five finalists: Olivia Echeverria, Hector Vargas-Perez, Kaila Sergent, Chantal Mortensen, and Jaime Lindow, competed for a unique prize, 1,000 gallons of gasoline! Jamie Lindow, a seventeen-year-old from Campbell, won with a rendition of a Celine Dion song.

Another first was a taping of "Taste of America" on Sunday for the Food Channel. Attempts had been made for the two previous years but never panned out. Mark Decarlo the host of the "Taste of America," was on stage for the taping. Ben Calvert, producer for the show, noted: "We've known about (the Garlic Festival) since our show started. It's a

world-renowned Festival." The show broadcasted the finals of the 2006 Gilroy Garlic Festival Great Garlic Cook-Off. Jennifer Malfas, a contestant from Orland Park, Ill., won the grand prize with "Oh Baby! Prosciutto Wrapped Roasted Garlic, Feta, and Rosemary Stuffed Bellas." It was Jennifer's first cooking competition and got her on the "Taste of America."

During an opening ceremony at the Garlic Cook-Off stage, Pirozzoli welcomed the crowd with a bit of trivia tailored

Attendance
90,280

What Was New

Garlic Idol Contest

$253K Non-Profits—28 Year Total: $7.5 Million

Garlic Chicken Caesar Salad Introduced

Demonstration Stage Enlarged

Taste of America Taped

Brian Bowe, New Executive Director

Volunteer of the Year

Lynn Liebschutz (Children's Area)

Queen Sheena Torres

HERBIE'S READY FOR ANY CULINARY TASK.

Gilroy Garlic Festival July 28, 29 & 30, 2006

Art Poster by JoAnne Robinson-Perez, Gilroy

Brian Bowe Brings High Tech Background to Festival

After an intensive five-month search, the Festival found just the right man to follow in the footsteps of the late Dick Nicholls as the Executive Director right under their noses—**Brian Bowe**, general manager of NP Expos Inc. in Morgan Hill.

Bowe was hired to manage the event that generated $2 million in revenue annually. His tasks ranged from funding to training and leading the over 4,000 community volunteers who feed, entertain and corral about 130,000 garlic-lovers who arrive from around the Bay Area and the globe.

Festival board member Jeff Martin, a Gilroy real estate investor and former president of the Festival, who was involved in the selection process, described Bowe as someone with relevant business and technical skills. His ten years of experience managing expos of up to 400 exhibitors and 15,000 attendees dovetailed with the executive director's duties.

Bowe was a friend to the prior Executive Director Dick Nicholls and brought the wisdom he had gleaned from that friendship to the job. He had volunteered when his wife chaired the finance committee and even his sweltering experience restraining a giant clutch of helium balloons one summer. Each experience gave him valuable insights into the task ahead.

"Is this good for the Garlic Festival and the community?" was one question that Mr. Nicholls often asked when faced with a difficult decision. Bowe vowed to keep that in mind as he began to accept the constraints and challenges of the job.

for some Mid-westerns. Quoting some interesting and outdated laws, she said: "In Gary, Indiana "it's illegal to go to a movie or ride public transportation within four hours of eating garlic. So don't go home too soon." Later in the day, Pirozzoli had one more piece of trivia to share: In Marianne, Oregon, a minister can't perform a service within an hour of eating garlic. "We would be quarantined for a month here in Gilroy," she said.

"I'm wiped out but ecstatic," Festival president Micki Pirozzoli said Sunday evening as she and dozens of event organizers kicked back and relaxed at the traditional post-Festival gathering. "I'm most excited about the great weather and how happy everyone seemed to be, from the volunteers to the vendors to the visitors."

"Anybody that's asked me how I do this, I say, "I don't do this. We do this,'" Pirozzoli said. "We're truly a family."

ABOVE: President Micki Pirozzoli lighting the flame on Friday.
UPPER RIGHT: putting it out on Sunday evening.
RIGHT: Molly Botill, Micki Pirozzoli, Frances Howson and Marcia Bodnar, Micki's mother.

Gourmet Alley 2006

The Board of Directors

Ed Struzik
Vice-President

Kirsten Carr
Secretary

George Minerva
Treasurer

Judy Lazarus
President

Micki Pirozzoli
Past President

Steve Padilla
Director

Rita Quintero
Director

Janie Mardesich
Director

Kurt Svardal
Director

Overall, the 2007 Garlic Festival was as good as it gets. The weather ordered by **Judy Lazarus**, Festival President, was perfect. She will tell you that she prayed every day leading up to the Festival for 85 degrees with a breeze. And she got it.

The weather was perfect, but attendance was also up, and happy visitors spent $200,000 more than the previous year. In addition, the new garlic fries in Gourmet Alley were a big hit, as was the Iron Chef Competition, and chef Guy Fieri kept the crowds entertained on the Cook-Off Stage.

The Gilroy Dispatch summed it up nicely: "A tip of the goofy garlic hat to President Judy Lazarus and every Gilroyan who helped lift the 2007 Festival to new heights. It's a fine thing, our fest; thanks for taking care of it."

Judy Lazarus, a paralegal, community leader, and Festival volunteer since 1988, was chosen to lead the 2007 Festival. She did it with grace and style. All weekend she wore a charm necklace with a sterling heart, a pea-size garlic bulb, and a heart she added this year as a testament to the Festival's love for all things garlic.

Lazarus didn't want the Festival to be a chore despite the increased responsibility as president.

"I want to enjoy it," she said. "I don't want to get to Sunday and say, 'What happened?' "

In her role, Lazarus had to work out logistics for several Festival additions, including moving garlic fries sales to Gourmet Alley, feeding volunteers there, and hosting a professional, Iron Chef-style battle. She, however, was confident that the details had been ironed out and that both Festival-goers and volunteers would be pleased with the changes.

"It's been nothing but a 100 percent fabulous experience," Lazarus said. ☙

Attendance
99,876

What Was New
Garlic Showdown

New Volunteer Rest Area

Meal Tickets for Gourmet Alley

Whiskey Falls on Vineyard Stage

Debut of Garlic Fries (Gourmet Alley)

Guy Fieri Hosted Garlic Recipe Contest

Volunteers of the Year
Margie Hemeon (Tickets)

Clyde Kreeger (Utilities)

Special Recognition
Bob Deal, Bob Gutierrez and Dave Sebold (Parking)

Queen Cherise Gowan

HERBIE'S IN FOR THE LONG HAUL; DONS GYM CLOTHES TO WIN THE RACE.

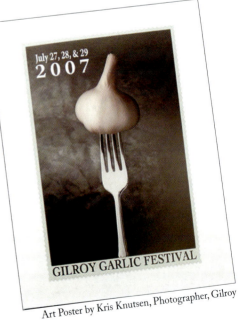

July 27, 28, & 29
2007
GILROY GARLIC FESTIVAL

Art Poster by Kris Knutsen, Photographer, Gilroy

"Garlic and More … in the Gilroy Area," was the title of a feature story in the summer 2007 edition of "RV Journal" that was available at Camping World in San Martin and other RV establishments throughout the western United States.

The story resulted from the Bay Area Travel Writers' Press Trip to Gilroy and Morgan Hill the previous fall.

The two-page story detailed the visit of writers Janet and Stuart Wilson to South County and described everything from the Garlic Festival, Andy's Orchard, LJB Farms, Guglielmo Winery, Gilroy Gardens, and other highlights of their trip to the area.

The press trip, hosted by the Gilroy Visitors Bureau and Morgan Hill Chamber of Commerce, was one of several regional marketing activities conducted through the "Gateway to the Central Coast" marketing campaign in 2006.

Promotion Brochure 2007 by J. Chris Mickartz

INTERESTING TIDBIT —

Garlic Fries added to Gourmet Alley Menu

In past years, Gordon Biersch had offered garlic fries but they did not submit an application in 2007. This opened the door for the Gourmet Alley chefs to come up with a winner. Gourmet Alley chairmen Alan Heinzen and Ken Fry cooked up the hit recipe with the help of willing taste-testers.

Festival's Iron Chef Competition

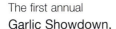

The first annual **Garlic Showdown,** scripted after "Iron Chef," a Food Network program in which contestants dive into a frantic culinary battle after learning the closely-guarded secret main ingredient(s) at the beginning of each show – an aspect Cook-Off organizers did not ignore.

A native of America's cousin across the Atlantic took home the honors and prize—a $5,000 check and, of course, 1,000 pounds of fresh Christopher Ranch gold.

Englishman Tony Baker, executive chef at Montrio Bistro in Monterey, wowed the five judges with his combination of garlic and artistry, serving them a stuffed pork tenderloin wrapped in pancetta and salmon on a roasted garlic potato galette.

"I'm absolutely bloody stoked," Baker said as he was presented the larger-than-life check to the accompaniment of his family cheering section.

Baker did not fail to give credit to sous chef Kirk Larsen as they jubilantly hugged following the announcement.

The four master chefs, sponsored by Bay Area radio stations, provided their own cookware, utensils, and spices for the tournament. But they did not know, until the stopwatch started ticking away the 75-minute prep time, what other ingredients they would be working with—except that garlic would play a major role.

"It was very tough," amateur judge Gene Sakahara said of the judging. "They were so creative. Their sauces were so flavorful, exquisite, and it was heavenly."

Fellow amateur judges Sam Bozzo, Don Christopher, Karen LaCorte, and Laura McIntosh were equally enthusiastic. However beyond the taste and artistic presentation, the judges had other essential criteria—garlic.

Celebrity Attention

Guy Fieri of Food Network's hit show "Guy's Big Bite" entertained the crowd during the Cook-Off Saturday. He also interviewed the Christophers of Christopher Ranch during a radio show from the Cook-Off stage. He jumped over the railing to visit contestants' spouses during the show, feed audience members gnocchi (one of the entrees), sign autographs, and pose for pictures. "Is this an awesome Festival or what?" he said.

Today, he is an American restaurateur, author, and Emmy Award-winning television presenter. By mid-2010, the Food Network had made Fieri the "face of the network". In 2010, The New York Times reported that Fieri brought an "element of rowdy, mass-market culture to American food television.

Garlic Idol

In its second year, the Garlic Idol competition was won by Gilroy Local, **Dominic Woodson.**

Dressed in a red shirt and tie, seventeen-year-old Woodson made the ladies scream with his song "Wait For You" by Elliot Yamin and his flashy moves. Woodson attended medical school and is currently an Orthopedic doctor with Doctors Medical Center in Modesto, CA. Singing is his hobby.

Sponsorships Afford Festival Community Impacts

By 2007, the Gilroy Garlic Festival Association had garnered company sponsorships worth a record $157,000 to use for major public improvement projects, such as the city arts center, public parks or joint high school facilities. The sponsorships, which connected company names with specific booths or events, were the highest total in Festival history and were added to past funds to create a pool of about $300,000, Executive Director Brian Bowe said.

"We tend to let some of that money accumulate so that we can have a bigger impact on the community," he said. "It gives us the ability to make special one-time improvements."

Separate from money raised by non-profits during the Festival, the sponsorship dollars go into an interest-bearing account created in 1998. They are not distributed to the organizations whose volunteers help run the event. In 2004, the Festival board of directors drew $250,000 from the account to construct the high school student center, which finished in 2006. The board also pledged $250,000 in 2005 for the Gilroy Cultural Arts and Performing Center, contributing about $150,000.

"We wouldn't be able to do (those large projects) if we distributed every last dollar to non-profits and charities that volunteered at the event," Bowe said.

Contributions include in-kind donations, such as garlic from Christopher Ranch, amenities booths like the Saint Louise Regional Hospital diaper-changing tent, and cash in exchange for having their brand put on an event like Nob Hill and the Garlic Showdown.

While the Festival reached a new high in sponsorship money, it has also increased its expenses through such events as the Garlic Showdown, which features professional chefs and a $5,000 prize. After expenses, the sponsorships will bring in about $112,000, the same net as last year. About $50,000 of this money will go toward continued support for the arts center.

The remaining $60,000 will pool with existing funds to create a total of about $300,000 to be distributed as the Festival board sees fit. However, the board has no date set to distribute these funds. Festival President Judy Lazarus said that the future project will be chosen from scores of applications and does not have to fit a mold or a specific time frame.

Since its inception, the Festival has spent more than $1.5 million from its sponsorship and general funds on public improvement projects. Those projects included $900,000 that was given in 1992 and 1996 for the purchase and improvement of ranchland which is now incorporated into Christmas Hill Park. Before 1998, contributions from the Festival's general fund dominated expenditures. In recent years, Bowe said that Festival organizers have leaned toward making sponsorship dollars a significant source of improvement projects.

While the new money has provided welcomed additions to the community, greed cannot drive the process, he said. Organizers do not want money to change the face of the Festival.

"We're always working on improving our relationship with sponsors and trying to increase our sponsors but we're very mindful of not over-commercializing the event. We want to maintain that small-town feel to the event."

Brian Bowe, Executive Director, Gilroy Garlic Festival Association

Dollars raised for local charities since 1979:
$7,571,105
The Gilroy Garlic Festival thanks you!

Val Filice 1927-2007

Remembering Gilroy's Legendary Garlic Festival Head Chef

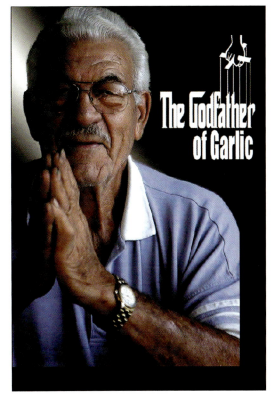

Val Filice passed away on November 4, 2007, losing his battle with cancer at 80 years of age. He was preceded in death by his wife Elsie in 1997. He was survived by his daughter, Valerie, son, Robert and three grandchildren.

When the Garlic Festival began in 1979, Valentino Filice farmed more than 200 acres of garlic between his family's land in Gilroy and land in San Joaquin Valley. He inherited the farming business and his passion for cooking from his parents, Angelina and Antonio, who moved to America from southern Italy in 1920.

The stinking bulb was a lifelong passion for Val, who said he fell in love with garlic a winter many years ago. "It was the only crop I saw with nice green rows," he explained. "I loved it and said to myself, 'Someday, I'm going to raise garlic.' And, I tried to raise the best garlic I could—and I raised some pretty good garlic."

Over the years, Filice and his brother grew a farming operation, but it was his mastery of the kitchen that secured his place as a founding father of the Gilroy Garlic Festival.

That culinary expertise was perfected in the "Tank House," a garden oasis and unofficial restaurant tucked out of sight on a cul-de-sac in south Gilroy. It was a cherished sanctuary for family and friends who congregated weekly to share stories over his famous cooking.

Although few had the chance to dine just steps from Filice's carefully planted rows of bell peppers, eggplants and tomatoes, hundreds of thousands of people have tasted his culinary creations over the years at the Garlic Festival.

Val was a larger-than-life, unassuming man, with a heart as big as all outdoors.. He had a presence you couldn't help but acknowledge. Everyone loved him. The media always wanted to interview Val. People wanted to take photos with him, although they weren't always quite sure why.

What some people may not know is that Val's culinary contributions over the years were not limited to the Festival. He also organized a crew of volunteer cooks to prepare dishes for homeless people at St. Joseph's Center during St. Patrick's Day and Thanksgiving. For over 20 years, he and his crew were invited to serve up garlic bread and other signature dishes at the AT&T Golf Tournament in Pebble Beach. A Christopher Ranch Christmas Party wouldn't have been the same without the Val crew cooking pepper steak sandwiches and pasta.

"Val was the Garlic Festival. He was the embodiment of community spirit. He never could say no. He cooked for any group that asked him and when word got out that Val was cooking, that event immediately became the place to be."

Don Gage
Past Mayor of Gilroy

ABOVE: Val overseeing Gourmet Alley at the 2007 Festival.

INSET: Bob Filice, Val's son, along with the other pyro chefs renamed the pyro area of Gourmet Alley "Val's Kitchen. May the flames be with you" in 2008.

FAR RIGHT INSET: One of the first photos available of Val mixing his famous pasta sauce for the very first Festival in 1979.

The Board of Directors

Kirsten Carr
Vice-President

Vince Whitmer
Secretary

Steve Padilla
Treasurer

Ed Struzik
President

Judy Lazarus
Past President

Janie Mardesich
Director

Lisa Sheedy
Director

Greg Bozzo
Director

Lonna Martinez
Director

The 30th Annual Festival was a hot one, averaging 91°, but a profitable one. **Ed Struzik** noted the financial power of heat. "The fact that it was so hot didn't hurt the bottom line at all," Struzik said.

It was a good year. Over the previous year, attendance at 107,553 was up 8 percent, as was overall income. Because of the heat, a big hit was the frozen lemonade and frosty bottles of water, generating $96,000. The 2008 Festival took in $2.2 million and gave $275K back to 169 non-profits.

Talking with Ed Struzik years after his year as a president, he regrets that he did not keep a journal. He remembers many great feelings but couldn't place the specifics years later. Overall, he noted that it was a great experience and that he marveled at the efficiency and level of "this amazing association." There were long lines at Gourmet Alley, but the volunteer crew kept the lines moving. There was a "bread emergency" as they ran out of bread and a few other essentials, but they managed to keep going. Ed remembers the three days of the Festival as an event managed by 4,000 remarkable volunteers who were in a constant "party first" mode.

Ed had a family emergency during the Festival. His daughter passed out due to the heat. While at the First Aide station, she was asked who her father was. She responded, " The President." The EMT was slightly startled and asked hesitantly, "George W. Bush?" She said "No, the Garlic Festival President, Ed Struzik!"

Ed recalled that besides the euphoria of the three days of the Festival, his most memorable day as President was in October 2008, when he signed 169 checks made out to the non-profits who worked the Festival.

2008 was also the first year for the Battle of the Bands competition. Five local groups, The Evince Expression, 51 Landmines, Exhibit A, The Beeftones, and Chasing Truth, qualified for the finals, and the Beeftones, from Hollister, took the top prize of $1,000. When the winners were announced, Tristan Kane, lead singer of Beeftones, shot his hands into the air and jumped up and down. The band consisted of Kane, drummer Geo Coelho, bassist Dean Fridman, and guitarist Michael Hardin.

Attendance
107,553

What Was New
Battle of the Bands

Fond Farewell to ShaBoom

Farewell to Garlic Godfather Val Filice

Festival Offices Move to New Building

20th Anniversary Takko Machi Relationship

Volunteer of the Year
Barbara Clark (Retail)

Queen Ariele Combs

HERBIE TAKES OVER THE ROLE OF MR. GARLIC.

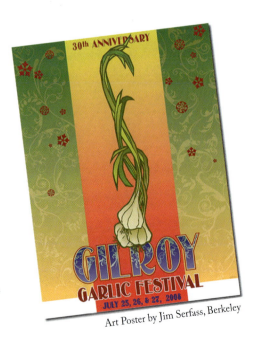
Art Poster by Jim Serfass, Berkeley

Festival Moves to New Offices

The Gilroy Garlic Festival Association moved into their new 4500 square foot offices at 7600 Monterey Street. The building, owned by the Festival, was dedicated to Richard "Dick" Nicholls, Festival Executive Director from 1986 to 2005. (See page 148).

"The Best Logo Poster EVER!" Ed Struzik, 2008 President
Design by J. Chris Mickartz, InfoPower Communications

Laura McIntosh, the star of a televised cooking program, emceed the July 26th Great Garlic Cook-Off finals, which Laura Benda of Madison, Wisconsin, won. Laura took top honors with a walnut-garlic tart with garlic-infused cream and chili syrup.

The SakaBozzo cooking team of Sam Bozzo and Gene Sakahara published a garlic cookbook to commemorate the 30th Gilroy Garlic Festival. "Any Bozzo Can Cook" features 102 garlic recipes.

Longtime Festival photographer, Bill Strange, celebrated his 25th year documenting the Festival. "I like the Cook-Off," Strange said. "Gourmet Alley is where it all happens. It's where a lot of the longtime volunteers are."

Bob Filice, son of the Garlic Godfather, Val Filice, along with the other pyro chefs, announced the renaming of the pyro area in Gourmet Alley. "Now it's called Val's Kitchen. May the flames be with you," Bob declared.

2008 Financials

Executive Director Brian Bowe gave some insights into the Garlic Festival finances.

"Our financial records are subject to an annual California Non-Profit Integrity Act Audit which we regularly pass with flying colors...We are significantly below the 20 to 30 percent national average for Festival administration costs."

Major Expenses % of Total:

Food & Beverages	12%
Administration	12%
Emergency Services	9%
Equipment Rental	6%
Marketing	6%
Grounds Preparation	5%
Souvenirs	4%
Liability Insurance	4%
Transportation	3.4%
Entertainment	2.4%

"Beyond the incredible food, the concerts and the children's area, the one underlying aspect of the Garlic Festival that has garnered this community international acclaim has been the annual work of our volunteers. It is the lifeblood of this event. Our Festival has been approached from all regions of this planet to learn how one community works together so well to make this celebration what it is."

Ed Struzik, President

162   THE GILROY GARLIC FESTIVAL PLAYBOOK *2008*

ShaBoom and that "Old Time Rock n' Roll!"

Back in 1981

— a group of high school teachers and a few musically inclined friends banded together to do a rock and roll benefit for the students at Independence High School in San Jose. The intent was to raise a little money for local sports and academic programs. Somehow the group clicked, and in 1981 the Gilroy Garlic Festival invited them to play.

Step Ahead Twenty Five Years

— they are retired educators/musicians, grandparents and are scattered around the states. But they pulled off one last performance at the 2008 Gilroy Garlic Festival. Don Christopher, Christopher Ranch, helped bring them to their first gig at the Festival in 1983 and then funded their scattered return in 2008! He noted, "They started here; they have to end here!"

During Their Heyday

— they played Festivals and benefits. They opened for bigger-name bands and became one of the go-to bands in the bay area for "Old Time Rock and Roll." They became the focal point for cruises and travel adventures and even played a gig on ABC television. And for 25 years, they were a featured highlight at the Garlic Festival. Some Festival visitors explain their reasons for visiting the Festival as "Pepper Steak sandwiches, garlic ice cream, and Shaboom." The San Jose Mercury News described ShaBoom as "a Festival's highlight."

Saying Goodbye

— 2007 was to have been the last year for ShaBoom to play at the Festival. But thanks to special arrangements by Don Christopher, the far-flung members of ShaBoom came back for one last gig at the 2008 Festival. The crowds danced, the band played their nostalgic mix, and everyone had a great time.

During their last performance at the Garlic Festival, several band members even had grandkids join them on stage. If you closed your eyes, ShaBoom's music was a bridge back to the 1981 Festival and the great music of the 50s and '60s, a time long before those grandkids!

John Dotson, lead vocals and a resident of Scottsdale, shouted out," Call me a relic, call me what you will. Say I'm old-fashioned. Say I'm over the hill. Today's music ain't got the same soul; I like that old-time rock 'n' roll."

"Thank you! You made a bunch of old guys really happy for 25 years!" lead singer Dee Quinet told a cheering, dancing crowd of nearly 1,000 people after he and his son, Brad Quinet, wrapped up "Old Time Rock n' Roll."

Members of ShaBoom:

John Dotson (Lead Vocals)
Retired after 36 years of teaching and coaching for the East Side Union High School District in San Jose.

Dee Quinet (Lead Vocals)
Retired after 35 years of teaching and coaching for ESUHSD

Mike Madden (Drums)
Retired from Lockheed Martin

Richard Zuniga (Saxophone)
Retired from Monterey County government

Dale Debruin (Keyboards and Lead Vocals)
Teaching for ESUHSD

Kevin McClure (Rhythm Guitar)
Maintenance Supervisor for Mount Diablo Unified School District in Concord

Mike Renwick (Lead Guitar)
Sales rep for Dean Markley Guitar

Celebrating 20 Years of Goodwill and Mutual Respect

2006 Takko Machi Garlic Lady and Mayor Al awaiting the flame-up, assisted by the Festival's pyro chefs.

Keiko Sato and friends from the Takko Machi Garlic Center wait for a flame up outside Gourmet Alley.

On stage, the 2007 Takko Machi Garlic Lady joins Gilroy Sister City representatives from France, Japan and Portugal.

The 30th Annual Gilroy Garlic Festival is an exceptional achievement, and not far behind that is the 20th anniversary of the establishment of Gilroy's Sister City relationship with Takko Machi, Japan. In 1988 Takko and Gilroy formalized the Sister City bond, and ever since, visitors from Takko have been regulars at the Garlic Festival. Current plans for 2008 anticipate a 20-member contingent from Takko Machi at the Festival.

It is not unusual for the Queen of the Takko Beef and Garlic Festival to be seen on the grounds of the Garlic Festival with the local Garlic Festival Queen. While Gilroy claims the title of Garlic Capital of the World, Takko Machi claims the title of Garlic Capital of Japan. Typically

Takko sends two contingents of students to Gilroy every year. In October, junior high students come, and high school students come in January. Annually, in early October, Gilroy sends a Festival and City contingent to Japan for their Garlic & Beef Festival. The Gilroy High School choir has visited Takko several times. An alumni choir group just wrapped up a visit to Takko.

In addition to these exchanges, Takko funds a Coordinator of International Relations (CIR) from the Gilroy area. College graduates apply for the position in Takko. Preliminary selections are made in Gilroy, while Takko makes the final selection. The CIR helps with English

classes in the Takko schools and serves as a liaison for the various exchange programs between the two cities.

In 2009 Gilroy Sister Cities established a scholarship/exchange program for some local high school students to spend time in Takko.

The Board of Directors

Greg Bozzo
Vice-President

Kurt Svardal
Secretary

Vince Whitmer
Treasurer

Kirsten Carr
President

Ed Struzik
Past President

Lisa Sheedy
Director

Ken Fry
Director

Lanny Brown
Director

Renee Harrigan
Director

Around the 31st Garlic Festival, the world was coming out of the great recession and a financial collapse. It had been a very tough year with many unknowns and negativity. President **Kirsten Carr**'s positive attitude was tasked to the limit as the Association wondered if anyone would come to the Festival and as they said goodbye to their new Garlic Festival building that was lost in the recession. But, as a lady who tested limits, she would press on and see a whopping 108,519 people attend.

As a young girl, she told her father, a staffer in the Kennedy White House, that she would be "The President." She even gave her father a dollar as a retainer for his political expertise! As an adult, with the presidency of the US not quite happening, she turned her sites to the presidency of the Garlic Festival and realized that goal in 2009. She notes that outside of having

two kids, the presidency of the Festival was her greatest accomplishment. Her memories of the Festival center around how under challenging times, the community rallied to put on an "amazing event."

She remembers the presidential reality setting is as she judged cars at the Chamber Car Show, had the opportunity to meet Steve Wozniak at a KRTY benefit, and welcomed the RVs at the Thursday night BBQ before the Festival. "I even got to meet the unofficial Mayor of Garlic Town in the RV area," she noted with a smile.

First-time Festival visitor and a six-year resident of Gilroy, John Larson, offered an interesting perspective: "The thing that got me was the enthusiasm and love of the Festival that I felt from the volunteers. They seemed to be having the time of their lives—from the people at the bike stand to the gate attendants, the food servers, the helpers wandering around. They love their Festival, and they are proud of it.

"You can't help your-self but love it right along with them. Of course, the other attendees enjoyed themselves, too, and that is probably a contributing factor to all the love I was feeling. But the volunteers have such pride in the whole thing that it all seems to stem from their passion, ensuring that everybody there has a good time. And

somehow, they manage to pull it all off without a hint of smugness."

On Sunday night, after President Carr extinguished the garlic bulb and was leaving the Park on a fire engine, she burst into tears, overcome with emotion and gratitude.

"I am so proud to be part of an event that includes thousands of volunteers working together to benefit the community while also throwing an incredible three-day party," said 2009 Festival President Kirsten Carr. "In a time when non-profits worry about keeping their doors open, we are thrilled to be able to assist them in helping others."

Attendance
108,519

What Was New
$240K Given to Non-Profits

Book Published Based on Festival

Festival Gets Facebook Page

First Festival without Val Filice and ShaBoom

Bicycle Parking Area

Volunteer of the Year
Tim Beckley (Home Depot Crew)

Queen Jessica Brewka

Art Poster by Ruth Johnson-Irving

Paella Takes Center Stage

In 2009, Paella was brought to the Festival by local caterer, Parsley, Sage, Rosemary & Thyme (Adam Sanchez). It added much to the already flavorful line-up. It was a fun spectacle, said Joann Kessler, the Festival's assistant executive director. The six-foot paella pan "was a sideshow in itself," she said. The paella station was located on the park side of Christmas Hill Park, near the Amphitheater.

The Gilroy Dispatch summed up the 31st Garlic Festival nicely:

"Festival Thirty-one-derful came off without a noteworthy hitch. The pepper steak sandwiches were better than ever, the calamari to die for, the weather perfect, and, most importantly, the crowds were healthy and happy. People left ready to spread the news about their good time on the last full weekend of July in Gilroy.

Gilroy should today pat itself on its collective back: Garlic mission accomplished."

INTERESTING TIDBIT —

Festival Inspired Book Released

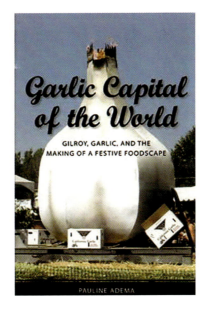

"I was just really captured by the community of Gilroy, the volunteerism, the huge success of the Festival and the impact the Festival had not only in the local community but also in the festival industry, which seems to look at Gilroy as the model of success. The city has created this fun, entertaining, marketable identity around this single food item."

Pauline Adema, Author

"Gilroy is a Mecca for garlic, and garlic lovers by the thousands make annual pilgrimages to the Gilroy Garlic Festival. Now aficionados can put the Garlic Festival into a broader cultural context, thanks to Pauline Adema's book. It is a must read for any absorbed by food festivals and a delicious read for everyone hooked on garlic!"

**Andrew F. Smith,
Author of Hamburger, A Global History**

Andrew Barth
Garlic Butter Cookies

The Board of Directors

Kurt Svardal
Vice-President

Shawn Keck
Secretary

Hugh Davis
Treasurer

Greg Bozzo
President

Kirsten Carr
Past President

Ken Fry
Director

Ed Mauro
Director

Lanny Brown
Director

George Minerva
Director

In 1979, **Greg Bozzo** was a junior high school student. He ran in the first Garlic Run and spent both days of the first Festival working in his father's minestrone soup booth. Papa and Mama Bozzo (aka Sam and Judy) were the owners of Digger Dan's, a restaurant on First Street at the time. It was really hot both days of the first Festival and making soup was not the best choice; it wasn't appealing to most people. The Festival was a hit, but the soup was not!

But for Greg, something happened that day; he got bitten by the Garlic Festival bug. And thirty-0ne years later, he is the president of the 2010 Festival.

At the second Gilroy Garlic Festival, the Bozzo's replaced the minestrone soup in favor of "steak on a stick." More favorably received, variations of the steak survived many future festivals. Greg was back at the Festival for the second, the third, and the fourth as a high school kid. He remembers convincing a group of bored friends that it would be "cool" to help out at the Festival. Some permanent friend-

ships developed among this "posse" of high school volunteers.

In the Festival's early days, there was a spirit of "just get it done." Greg remembers painting old wooden booths, cutting frozen calamari on band saws at the old Albertsons, and peeling garlic till his hands had a permanent odor of the stinking rose! Even in his college days at Cal Poly, San Louis Obispo, Greg managed to get home and work the Festival.

Since those early days of volunteering anywhere and everywhere, Greg has taken leadership roles in Hospitality, Information, the Cook Off-Stage, and Gourmet Alley. After a short break from active participation at the Festival, he was elected to the Board of Directors, then chosen to reign as the 2010 President. This experience has

shaped one of Greg's major perspectives on the Festival — the early founders saw it and built it into the governance of the Festival. Leadership roles in the Festival are temporary positions. The idea is to work as a chairperson, board member, or officer (each for a couple of years) and then move on. The Festival does not have a place for permanent, lifelong positions. In Greg's mind and the founders' intent,

INTERESTING TIDBIT —

The Garlic Festival Goes Green

The Garlic Festival began a mission to make the event earth friendly with a three year campaign to produce a zero-waste event. They identified traditionally regarded garbage that could be designated as a valuable resource instead of waste by working with food vendors to ensure that produces used with food could be composted and designated vendors who agreed to use compostable utensils as "Green Garlic" vendors. They then established Recycling Booths in strategic locations throughout the grounds for composting, recycling and trash. As a final effort, they encouraged folks to ride their bikes to the Festival by providing a bicycle parking area.

Art Poster by Peggy Dean, Gilroy

Attendance
97,667

What Was New

$270K Given to Non-Profits

Campaign to Produce Zero Waste

Volunteers of the Year
Joanne and Joe Curro (Recipe Contest)

Queen Lauren Iwanaga

Greg Bozzo manning his parents booth at the first Gilroy Garlic Festival in 1979.

Greg with his father Sam Bozzo and friends Shawn & Derek Johnson at the second Garlic Festival, held at Christmas Hill Park.

Greg with students in Takko Machi during his first experience there in 1991.

Greg running in the Garlic Fun Run at the first Festival.

At age 19, Greg worked with Bert Berry (l) and Chris Sullivan (r) at Hospitality—marking the beginning of his official involvement in the Festival.

During a trip to Kyoto in the Fall of 1999, Greg met Lora, his wife.

this is a good thing in that it brings new blood and spirit to an organization that can sap one's creativity and energy or creates dynasties.

In 1990 Sam Bozzo was President of Gilroy Garlic Festival XII; in 2010, son, Greg Bozzo is the President of Gilroy Garlic Festival XXXII. Greg feels strongly that one of the strengths of the Garlic Festival is its "staying power." The Festival can reinvent itself annually with new leadership while staying true to its history and traditions. Every year the Festival becomes more efficient while it has to contend with costs and issues that did not exist ten, twenty, or thirty years ago. Health, security, fire safety, insurance, and liability requirements and expenses increase annually. Without better efficiency without more stringent controls on costs, the Festival could not continue.

Sustainability is one of Greg's goals for the XXXII Festival and future Festivals, which is a return to its roots. The early Festivals used local and regionally supplied food. While Greg realizes that sustainability might be "pie in the sky," it is a worthy goal and keeps an eye on the future. It is suitable for the region. Sustainability is not a vote for uber- provincialism — it is

a shot at using local, regional, nationally produced foods. Some of the focus areas are California-grown garlic, Watsonville mushrooms, California olive oil, San Francisco-made pasta, local wineries, Northern California chickens, regional beef, local vegetables, and domestic wild shrimp.

The Festival is for and about the people from this area, region, and nation in spite of the increase in costs that might occur. Greg and Festival organizers have been able to convince some local, regional or national vendors who had higher prices to trade the difference for publicity and Festival exposure.

Sustainability is also about less plastic, styrofoam, garbage, and more compostable recyclable materials. Vendors are encouraged to get on the sustainability bandwagon by competing for a "Green Garlic Award' which is presented to the vendor who has demonstrated the most sustainable practices during Garlic Festival XXXII. A group of special-needs children will remove bottle caps from plastic bottles and garner a little recycling money.

Local news has played up the cost

of the Festival's environmental impact on Uvas Creek. While this is a costly issue, it is a necessary one. It is part of the sustainability of the more significant problem.

The Garlic Festival has shaped Greg's life. Because of the Garlic Festival, Gilroy acquired a Sister City in Takko Machi, Japan. Because of the sister cities relationship Takko established, a Coordinator of International Relations (CIR) afforded a Gilroy resident the opportunity to live and work in Takko. Greg spent two years in Takko, where he met his wife, Lora. She returned to Takko as a CIR a few years later. Takko and Lora led to marriage, two daughters, and a house on Hanna Street. Working at the Garlic Festival also led to a commitment to community service. All this, together with visits to Angra, Gilroy's Portuguese Sister City, and Monticelli, Gilroy's Italian Sister City, and a garlic cooking competition in Edmonton, Canada, has shaped Greg's perception of the world.

This gardner/landscape designer, long-time Festival volunteer, and local family man is connected to his community and the world in a unique way. And, it can be attributed to the Festival! 🧄

The Board of Directors

Hugh Davis
Vice-President

Ken Fry
Secretary

Dennis Harrigan
Treasurer

Kurt Svardal
President

Greg Bozzo
Past President

Shawn Keck
Director

Ed Mauro
Director

Lanny Brown
Director

Susie Bible
Director

By 2011, the country had survived the 2008-09 recession, and the economy was looking up. Things were looking good for Gilroy's annual Festival, and for President **Kurt Svardal,** the focus was to improve the finances of the Festival.

For Svardal, it was "A great Festival. It flowed well. For many of the long-time volunteers, it was the 'funnest' Festival." He marveled that the harder the volunteers worked, the more fun they had! He remembers that he went into Gourmet Alley on the Monday after the Festival to find the volunteers sitting around—literally exhausted—unable to get anything done. So he went around the Festival grounds and gathered ten people to go to Gourmet Alley to help out. Later, when he went by, he found the formerly exhausted volunteers and the recruits getting the cleanup done, having a great time!

2011 marked the first year that the

Association made its presence known on social media. It was also the first time visitors would be able to order Gourmet Alley combo plates online before the Festival. This ordering system had a few kinks but gave the Festival organizers some insight into the amount of food needed. It proved invaluable on Sunday morning when the pre-ordered meals numbers were checked. They found that not all of the pre-orders were redeemed. As Svardal entered Gourmet Alley, he heard Vito Mercado, chair of the Alley, ordering additional food for the day. He interrupted Vito's call to tell him about the number of outstanding online orders. Vito immediately got back on the phone and told his supplier: "Give me ALL the calamari you have!"

Later in the afternoon Gourmet Alley was running out of bread. Shoppers were dispatched to local supermarkets. As a result, Nob Hill Foods was out of French bread for several days.

Almost $300,000 was given back to local non-profits in 2011, for a total of $9,345,322 back to local non-profits since 1979. Attendance was 109,067, and total income was $2.15 million.

An interesting contrast can be found in comparing Festival technology in 1979 and 2011. In 1979 the primary technology outreach was on KFAT, a local renegade radio station. Thirty-three years later, it was all about Facebook and Twitter. The 2011 Festival had 15,465 Facebook "Likes," 7,800 Facebook visitors, and on July 30, it was trending on Twitter! 🧄

Attendance
109,067

What Was New
$290K Given to Non-Profits

$9,345,322 to Non-Profits Since 1979

Shrimp & Steak Wrap Introduced

Chef Angelo Sosa, a Michelin Star winner and Top Chef participant performed

Volunteers of the Year
Bill Hart and Bill Ung (Gourmet Alley)

Queen Tiffani Peterson

Shrimp & Steak Wrap

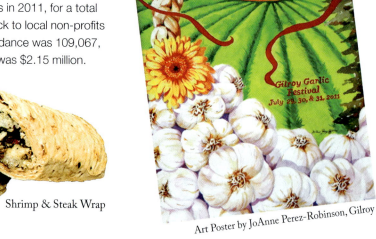
Art Poster by JoAnne Perez-Robinson, Gilroy

The Renovation of the Amphitheater

The approximately $350,000 worth of renovations included:

- Wooden seating, dirt walkways replaced by concrete and sod

- Retaining walls removed and replaced by keystone

- Construction of 6,650-square-foot shade structure over seating area

- Installation of sound mixing stage in middle of seating area

- Installation of electrical conduits for future lighting options

- New shade fabric coverings

President Kurt Svardal addresses the Association Thursday evening before Festival 2011.

Bill Ayer (1981 President) and Norie Goforth (1983 President) were welcome visitors at the 2011 Festival.

INTERESTING TIDBITS —

Target Ad Features Festival

TV advertisement for Target featured two people eating a generic "garlic ice cream" at an equivocal "Garlic Festival." The ad had Gilroyans singing praises for their hometown; leaving comments on YouTube such as "born and raised in Gilroy" and "the timing of this commercial couldn't have been better, July 29th, 30th, 31st, See you there!"

Gilroy Dispatch Praises the Festival Volunteers

The local paper gave huge kudos to volunteer President Kurt Svardal and to every Gilroyan who made the Festival happen. "It sounds cliché —and it is—but it's true. There are volunteers working as you read who are finishing the tear down—tough sledding after the festivities are over. There are volunteers who tracked down supplies of calamari when the crowds overwhelmed—in spite of optimistic ordering. There are volunteers who served water to guests waiting in long lines for combo plates—it's all about hospitality."

Traditions

Although the Festival is ever-changing, there are some traditions that have stood the test of time. Some of those are represented in the photos on the next few pages: 1) 2011 President Kurt Svardal lights the garlic bulb marking the official beginning of the 33rd Annual Gilroy Garlic Festival, 2) Festival Queen Tiffani Petersen hands the torch to Mr. Garlic, Gerry Foisy, 3) It wouldn't be a Garlic Festival without the infamous garlic steak sandwich and 4) Festival committee chairs and co-chairs, at their last official meeting (held at the newly renovated amphitheater), on the Wednesday before the Festival began.

2011

Like magic, each last full three-day weekend in July, Christmas Hill Park is transformed into a home that hosts over 100,000 people. Over 4,000 volunteers treat their guests to food, drink, shopping, entertainment and fun. The 33rd Annual Gilroy Garlic Festival was more than just a huge success in numbers and dollars raised. It was another triumph for the community. A time when neighbors joined neighbors to work for their favorite non-profit organization. It was a time for friends who hadn't seen each other all year to catch up. And it was a time to introduce people from all over the world to the beautiful community that we call home.

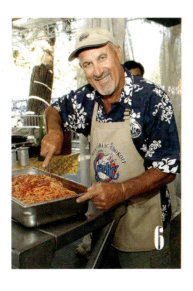

5) Hungry volunteers stand in line on the Thursday before the Festival in Gourmet Alley, where they are treated to a pasta dinner complete with pasta, salad, fruit and garlic bread. Martin McAvoy (Pyro Chef during the Festival) joined Patty Gravell and Judy Filice serve. 6) Bobby Filice, son of the late Val Filice (one of the founders of the Festival), fills his father's shoes as head chef of the Thursday volunteer dinner.

Scampi | Calamari | COMBO TWO
GARLIC SAUSAGE SANDWICH
CHICKEN STIR FRY & SCAMPI | COMBO ONE
PEPPER STEAK SANDWICH
PENNE CON PESTO & CALAMARI

1) Jamie Brown-Miller from Napa, winner of the Great Garlic Cook-Off, prepares her award-winning dish, Stacked Napoleon on Garlic Paper with Asparagus, Radicchio, Shitakes and Stilton.

2) Gourmet Alley had a record number of sales over the three days.

3) Queen Tiffany Petersen and her court braiding garlic, helped by Elaine Bonino.

4) Brittany Nielsen, KSBW8 interviews Steve Janich, Pyro Chef as he preps calamari for flame up.

5) Pat DeStasio from Christopher Ranch has been managing the Christopher booth at the Festival since the very first one in 1979.

Behind the Scenes

Volunteers work behind the scenes to make the Garlic Festival such a huge success:

1) Tim Fredricks, Hub & Pub (Volunteer Hospitality). 2) John Tomasello, Glenita Gordon and David Franklin, Cook-Off Stage Set-Up. 3) Attorney Bill Gates, began his involvement with writing the original Articles of Incorporation for the Festival 34 years ago. 4) Denise Turner and Dale Foster, Gilroy Rotary Wine Pavilian Set--up. 5) Pam Martin, Gilroy Foundation Wine Cooler Booth. 6) Jennifer Wanzong, Children's Area Chairwoman. 7) Chipper Perkins, Cook-Off Stage Clean-Up. 8) Irene Unenoto, Pepper Steak Sandwiches. 9) Keg Rollers Kyle Wanslow, Robert Carrera, and Dan Sterner, Chamber Beer Concession.

1) John Torres, Pepper Steak, graduated from Gilroy High School. 2) Robert Deal hanging sign, also built the kitchen counter/units for Garlic Cook-Off area. 3) Nicole Spence (12 years old), two-fistedly doles out water to thirsty Festival-goers. 4) Gilroy High School Basketball volunteers. 5) Volunteers assemble steak sandwiches. 6) Pasta server, Dolores Diaz from San Jose, works with friends each year.

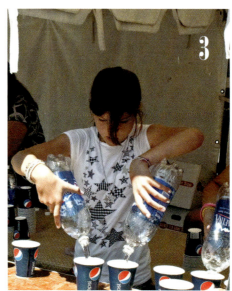

Faces

7) Todd Trekel with his mother Barbara. Todd began working at the Festival in 1993 helping his mother in the lemonade booth, then programs. 8) Trekell working with Personnel in Gourmet Alley—instructing volunteers.

9) Georgia Garfink checks ID's at Gilroy Chamber of Commerce beer ticket booth. 10) Festival goer enjoying the pepper steak sandwich. 11) Official Festival photographer, Bill Strange with Mrs. & Mr. Garlic, Jeanne & Gerry Foisy at the President's party immediately following the end of the Festival on Sunday.

1) First-time Festival attendee, Sarah Reyes, holds up garlic from the Garlic Braiding Contest. 2) Festival supporter, Frank Angelino (Gilroy). 3) Robert Mendez (Gilroy). 4) Kevin Coyle (Los Gatos) and Claire Cheng (Santa Clara) with garlic ice cream. 5) Clyde Kreeger, 11-year volunteer helps out in Utilities. He comes all the way from Gila Bend, Arizona to help out. 6) Elissa Shaffer, just 6-years-old, enjoying ice cream at the Cooking Demo area.

Special Thanks to Special People

Don & Karen Christopher

Majid Bahriny

Executive Director Brian Bowe

President Kurt Svardal

Don (Founder) & Karen Christopher generously support the Festival at every turn. Their major contribution this year made the renovation of the Amphitheater possible.

Majid Bahriny, Mama Mia's, a huge supporter of the Festival and host of the President's dinner, came through in a big way when Gourmet Alley ran out of steak and calamari on Saturday.

President Kurt Svardal put in countless hours making sure that guests to the Festival would have a wonderful time.

Executive Director Brian Bowe is the glue that holds it all together throughout the year. He always goes above and beyond the call of duty .

Festival Grounds, Sunday, July 31, 10 pm

And we said good night and see you again next year to the best party in the world,

The Gilroy Garlic Festival

Recipe Submission

The nine-month process begins in November when the "Cook-Off" Chairperson, this year, Deanna Franklin, and core group of volunteers start the planning process. By December, the call for recipes goes out. May 1st was the 2012 deadline. Over 120 submissions were received! As soon as recipes start coming in, the chair and core group vote "yes," "no," or "maybe" on each recipe. "Maybe" submissions are given a second review at the next monthly meeting. By mid-May 60 recipes are sent on for further review.

UPPER LEFT: Shane Fuller joins her friend and fellow foodie, Wendy Brodie at her home to prepare several of the recipes that make it into the test stage of the competition. LEFT: Barbara Orth, Glenita Gordon and J. Chris Mickartz help prep the ingredients for recipes as well.

The Anatomy of a Garlic Festival Cook-Off

Reviews & Test

In this next phase, Wendy Brodie, well know Central Coast executive chef, artist, author, TV food show host, and restaurant owner, reviews each of the recipes. Contestants with more than one submission are asked to pick one. Professional chefs and food critics are eliminated. Finally about 20 recipes are selected for a test cook. Wendy and her husband, Robert Bussinger convert their home into a test kitchen. Volunteers from Gilroy travel to the Brodie home to actually cook the recipes. At this point, recipes are judged on the clarity and precision of the recipe directions, looks and taste. By June 13, Wendy whittles the 20 down to eight finalists who are then invited to compete in the 2012 "Cook-Off" on Saturday, July 28.

2012 Finalists

Greek Fisherman's Dream, Savory Garlic Pistachio BAKLAVA
with Balsamic Reduction and Sea Scallops — **Susan Mason/Milton, WA**

Creamy Bacon Mushroom & Spinach Accordion RAVIOLI
— **Karen Harris/Castle Rock, CO**

For The Love Of Garlic Chicken Potato HASH on a Trio of Sauces
—**Teresa Hargrove/Lawton, OK**

Golden Garlic Chicken-Broccoli Rabe LASAGNA CUPS with Fiery Roasted Jalapeno
Alfredo Sauce and Red Chili Oil — **Veronica Callaghan/Glastonbury, CT**

Roasted Garlic TAMALES with Bacon Garlic Jam
— **Jennifer Beckman/Falls Church, VA**

Garlic Lamb MEATBALLS in Indian Spiced Sauce over Coconut Garlic Infused Rice
— **Renee Pokorny/Ventura, CA**

Crispy PORK BELLY with Caramelized Onion, Fig Agrodolce and Creamy Polenta
— **Laureen Pittman/Riverside, CA**

Triple Garlic Mini CHEESECAKES — **Janice Benthin/Montreal, QC, Canada**

ABOVE LEFT: Erin Monroe, Glenita Gordon, Valerie Marinovich, and Todd Jones prepare gift boxes for contestants.

ABOVE RIGHT: Hosts Chris & Kim Ordaz welcome Canadian contestant Janice Bethin and her friend, Dorothy Dodd, to dinner held in the contestants' honor on the Friday of the Festival.

RIGHT: Rita Quintero, Phylis Mantelli and Natalie Sanchez prepare the dishes for the judges.

BELOW: Celebrity emcee Kate Callahan poses with Chairperson, Deanna Franklin just before the announcement of the 2012 Gilroy Garlic Festival Cook Off winner.

This year, the eight finalists came from six states and Canada; as close as Riverside and Ventura to as far away as Montreal and Connecticut. Finalists receive an air, car and hotel stipend. Arriving on Friday they are hosted to a welcome dinner Friday evening. At the dinner they are introduced to one of the most coveted positions at the Gilroy Garlic Festival, chaperone to a "Cook Off" finalist. Chaperones serve as sous-chef, companion, local shopper, "go to" person, coach and supporter.

There is a great story from a few years back. One finalist was so overwhelmed by the crowds, media and attention that she started shaking so badly she could not cook. The chaperone stepped in and finished her dish according to her instructions!

A Special Thank You
Jan Bernstein Chargin for letting us use her beautiful garlic illustration.

The Day of the Event ...

Saturday morning the finalists are on stage by 8 am. "Cook-Off" rules say that the entrée must be prepared in two hours or less. At 10:30 am, the first recipe is plated and ready for judging. By 12:15 pm, the winner is identified. The 2012 judges were:

Jay Minzer – Private Chef, New York
Luca Rutigliano – Executive Chef, CordeValle Resort
Evelyn Miliate – Raley's, Bel Air, Nob Hill Foods
Majid Bahriny – Mama Mia's Restaurant
Wendy Brodie – Food Consultant, Art of Food TV

Recipes are judged on six criteria:

Ease of preparation
Flavor
Texture
Creativity
Appearance
Use of Garlic

In 1979, at the first Gilroy Garlic Festival, the first "Cook-Off" winner, Kelly Green of Mill Valley, would hardly recognize the event today. The original "Cook-Off" was held at Gavilan College. There were only a few spectators and not much fanfare for Kelly's Asian Chicken.

Today, the "Cook-Off" is a big-time production that starts in November and culminates on Saturday of the Festival with a garlic crown, a $1,000 prize, a stadium crowd, TV coverage, celebrity judges and paparazzi!

TOP: Judges Evelyn Miliate, Wendy Brodie, Majid Bahriny and Luca Rutigliano discuss an entry in front of crowd and cameras. **ABOVE**: Celebrity emcee, Dan Green, interviews Susan Mason from Milton, Washington as she plates her Savory Garlic Pistachio Baklava with Balsamic Reduction and Sea Scallops for the judges. The stage was alive with media from all over the Bay Area.

The Winning Recipe

Crispy Pork Belly with Caramelized Onion, Fig Agrodolce and Creamy Polenta

Serves 7 to 8 people.

The Winner
Laureen Pittman
from Riverside, CA

INGREDIENTS:

Pork Belly
2 rectangular slabs pork belly (1½ - 2 pounds each),
 (remove the skin only-leave the fabulous fat!)
4 tablespoons kosher salt
2 tablespoons coarse ground pepper
1 head garlic, cloves separated, unpeeled
1 quart chicken broth

Agrodolce Sauce
2 tablespoons extra-virgin olive oil
1 large yellow or brown onion, chopped (about 1½ cups)
3 cloves garlic, minced or pressed
½ cup balsamic vinegar
½ cup dry red wine
½ cup apple juice
½ cup honey
7 ounces dried figs, tough stems removed and chopped
1 teaspoon fresh chopped rosemary
½ teaspoon salt
½ cup water (if necessary)

Polenta
4 cups chicken stock
4 cups whole milk
2 teaspoons salt
2 cups polenta (not quick-cooking) or yellow cornmeal
½ cup heavy cream
½ cup shredded Parmigiano-Reggiano
Water, if necessary

8 sprigs fresh rosemary, for garnish

METHOD OF PREPARATION:

Pork Belly Score the fat of the pork belly without cutting into the meat. Rub the salt and pepper onto both sides of the slab. Place the slabs, fat side up, in a 10-12 quart pressure cooker (in a singe layer if possible - you can cut them in half, if needed), then pour the chicken broth over the top of the belly. Throw in the unpeeled garlic cloves. Lock the lid on the pressure cooker. Bring the pressure cooker up to high pressure, and then lower the heat to maintain that pressure and cook for 45 minutes. Remove from the heat and allow the pressure to come down naturally, 15 to 20 minutes. Remove belly from braising liquid, along with the garlic cloves; drain and keep warm.

Agrodolce Sauce While the pork belly is in the pressure cooker, make the agrodolce sauce. Heat the olive oil in a large, deep skillet (12-inch) over medium-high heat, add onions and sauté 15-20 minutes, stirring occasionally, until golden and tender. Add the minced garlic and cook, stirring constantly, for another 30 seconds. Stir in remaining ingredients and bring to boil over high heat. Reduce heat to medium-low and cook, stirring occasionally, until mixture is thickened and syrupy, 30-40 minutes. Keep warm. Add water, a little at a time, if sauce becomes too thick.

Polenta While finishing the agrodolce, start the polenta. Bring the broth, milk and salt to a boil in a 4-quart heavy pot, then add polenta in a thin stream, whisking. Cook over moderate heat, whisking, 2 minutes, to prevent lumps. Reduce heat to low and simmer polenta, covered, stirring every 10 minutes or so, 45 minutes total. Add the cream and the Parmigiano-Reggiano. Remove from the heat and keep warm until ready to serve. Stir occasionally and check for seasoning. Add salt and pepper, if necessary, and stir in a little water if polenta thickens too much.

To serve, cut the pork belly into 7 or 8 serving pieces. Sear the fat side of the belly in a hot, non-stick skillet or griddle until crispy (45 seconds to 1 minute). Be careful not to burn the fat. Spoon some of the warm polenta onto a serving plate. Top with a piece of the crispy pork belly and a spoonful of the agrodolce. Squeeze a couple of the cooked garlic cloves out of their skins and on top of the agrodolce. Garnish with a sprig of fresh rosemary.

SAN FRANCISCO GIANTS GAME

Presented by the Garlic Festival Association

On June 21, 2013 the Gilroy Garlic Festival Association hosted the Second Annual Giants Garlic Festival at Seals Plaza just outside AT&T Park. The beautiful afternoon was a perfect backdrop as hundreds of orange and black garlic fans sampled Gilroy's own garlic fries along with the Festival's newest dish, zesty garlic fried calamari. Hard-working Festival volunteers kept things moving to make sure everyone was well fed. Special guests included the Garlic Festival queen and court, Mr. Garlic, and Giants manager Bruce Bochy. Guests left with a custom tin of mints to help during the game and on the ride home.

Giants announcer, Marty Lurie, shares his world series ring, for a moment, with Greg Gordon.

The Board of Directors

Vito Mercado
Vice-President

Deanna Franklin
Secretary

Mike Wanzong
Treasurer

Dennis Harrigan
President

Hugh Davis
Past President

Judy Lazarus
Director

Steve Padilla
Director

Mike Zukowski
Director

Randy Costa
Director

Standing just in front of the famed flaming garlic bulb near the park entrance on the first day of the 35th Garlic Festival, President **Dennis Harrigan** appeared to be enjoying himself, beaming: "we're going to have a great Festival."

And a great Festival it was. A record $350,000, benefiting 167 organizations were made possible by the 2013 Festival's financial success. And another $248,000 were available for Christmas Hill Park improvements that included the Mulberry Picnic area, new trees on the Ranch side, and the enlargement of the turn-around area from the accumulative sponsorship funds collected over the years.

As with most successes in life, it was a winning combination of luck and planning. The luck came in the form of mild weather, Majid Bahriny's new garlic-fried calamari dish, the garlic train that brought a host of Peninsula visitors, and the introduction of some new technologies (a new smart-phone app) to help navigate the Festival.

President Harrigan likes to cook and readily admits that he thought he "had arrived" when he prepared a Chicken Etoufée on the demonstration stage for more than 100 spectators in the early 90s. A question from a female spectator in the audience: "How do you make it vegetarian?" He had to pause for a second and just happened to look down at a local newspaper clipping listing the schedule of events and realized why he received such an out-of-left-field question. He politely pointed out that he was a local Veterinarian, not a Vegetarian.

As president in 2013, the veterinarian Harrigan received a call on his official Garlic Festival radio that he was needed in First Aid. A dog was experiencing a heat stroke. At first, he thought maybe some board member(s) were spoofing him again. He had been summoned to First Aid once before with a report of a horse needing stitches. That time, there was no horse, no stitches required. Although suspicious, he went to the First Aid area to find a dog that indeed was experiencing a heat stroke. After about an hour of doctoring and some intravenous fluids, the dog and owner were able to move on, hydrated, and ready to continue to enjoy the Festival.

Harrigan's first volunteer gig in 1989 was handing out water bottles, along with his wife of 34 years, as part of the fundraising efforts for Rod Kelley Elementary School, where his two sons, Brian and Kyle, went to school. 🧄

HERBIE CHILLS OUT AT THE 2013 FESTIVAL.

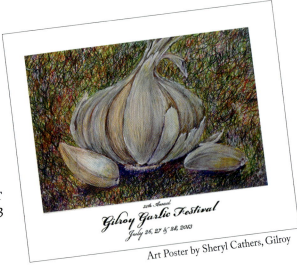

Gilroy Garlic Festival
July 26, 27 & 28, 2013

Art Poster by Sheryl Cathers, Gilroy

Pigs in the Park with Garlic, a Hit

Ribs glazed in olive oil and garlic and smoked in hickory and oak wood was just one of the concocted recipes for the first-ever "Pigs in the Park with Garlic" barbecue rib Cook-Off Friday at the 35th Annual Gilroy Garlic Festival.

The all-new cooking contest was the brainchild of John Melone, son of Garlic Festival co-founder Rudy Melone. John, along with the Garlic Festival committee, selected the top four professional Bay Area barbecue crews to compete in the contest.

Myles McEntee, owner of Catering by Five, along with his daughter took the first place trophy. McEntee had served as head chef of the San Jose Sharks for the last 16 years,

"It's a rotten job, but someone has to do it!"

The annual Gilroy Garlic Festival is a huge undertaking with plenty of media-worthy stories and pictures. We have all seen photos of calamari flame-ups, the queen and her court, Cook-Off winners, and celebrity visitors. All these people are deserving of recognition and are part of what makes the Garlic Festival so special.

Not often photographed and rarely the subject of media stories are some remarkable hard working volunteers—the people of refuse and transportation. Both groups use a lot of volunteers and handle some logistical nightmares.

Ryan MacPhail, a college student by day, is the Chair of Refuse. Following Recology's direction, the stuff 102,000 people leave behind is not trash but recyclable refuse. This year, for the first time, the Garlic Festival set out to recycle as much as possible. Mostly gone were the Garlic Festival trademark tan cardboard barrels. Refuse containers were colored blue for recycled plastic, glass, cardboard and cans. Compost refuse containers were green. All serving trays, plates and utensils used during the Garlic Festival were compostable or recyclable.

The job of refuse starts the week before the Festival with the prepping of containers, distribution, and setting up the collection station behind the Vineyard stage. During the Festival, volunteers from the local wrestling groups, basketball teams and New Hope Community Church emptied full containers and replace them with fresh ones. In past years tractors with refuse trailers actually patrolled the grounds. This year, as a safety precaution for Festival visitors, the tractors and trailers were restricted to the periphery of the Festival Grounds. Friday with the smaller crowds went well but Saturday, with the largest crowds, turned into a refuse overflow situation. The volunteers just could not get onto the grounds on foot fast enough to keep the refuse from piling up. Sunday refuse went back to patrols on the grounds.

According to Phil Couchee, General Manager at Recology, the local waste management facility, about 88 tons of trash were removed from the grounds with almost 30 percent of that going to recycle or composting. He did not have data on the amount of bottles with CRV value that were also recovered. Festival-

goers helped with the process by using the appropriate containers. Refuse volunteers worked hard to keep everything separate, and, finally, Recology staff like Julie Alter, Wastezero Specialist, did some final sorting.

At night after each Festival day, an interesting phenomenon occurs. Volunteers from Gilroy Gaters sweep the whole park grounds for leftover refuse. By Monday morning it is hard to believe 102,000 people wandered through the 50 acres of Christmas Hill Park.

Hats off to the volunteers, to Recology, to the Festival Board and to Refuse Chairman Ryan MacPhail and his Vice Chair, Dan Gilleland for pushing the Festival to a greener place. (Ryan & Dan, photo center left, page 22.)

Ryan and Dan offer another example of the diversity of the Festival Leadership. Ryan will soon return to college in Washington and retire from Refuse leadership while "retiree" Dan Gilleland will take over. At the Festival, leadership is not measured by years on this planet, but by the willingness to volunteer and the ability to get the job done!

"Overall there was an increase in recycling tonnages (including organics). I think people are more conscious of where they put their waste, and they generally want to recycle. The fact that more recycling and organics containers were available to the public helped give them more opportunities to divert their waste. The combination of the efforts of the attendees, the volunteers that emptied the containers and the sorting of the recyclables, helped increase the recycling weights."

Julie Alter, Wastezero Specialist, Recology

The Board of Directors

Deanna Franklin
Vice-President

David Reynolds
Secretary

Gwyneth Sauceda
Treasurer

Vito Mercado
President

Dennis Harrigan
Past President

Brent Jenkins
Director

Randy Costa
Director

Kurt Svardal
Director

Jim Buessing
Director

The Gilroy Garlic Festival faced and overcame some significant challenges in 2014. It was stinky hot Friday and Saturday, and then it rained on Sunday! The cautionary weather reports kept a lot of people away. In addition, it was the first year the Festival had to deal with off-site parking and the associated costs, jumping from $70,000 to $200,000.

Vito Mercado, the Garlic Festival President for 2015, noted, "We had some unusually warm weather this weekend, but we still shined." "I'm like the number one fan, the number one cheerleader," the Gilroy native said. "The President can't do it all by himself; it's all because the volunteers work so well together and have been volunteering for years and years. My job is to cheer them on and stay out of everybody's way to accomplish the goals they have set out to accomplish."

New for the 36th annual Festival was the installation of a robust Wi-Fi system that allowed vendors to process payments and transactions much more efficiently. There was also the introduction of the first three-day pass for locals.

The Cooking competitions were fast and furious over the three-day Festival. The Garlic Bowl II pitted three university cooking teams against each other. Santa Clara University with Executive Chef Josh Grimes and his sous chef Mark McGowan defeated teams from Fresno State and Cal Berkeley.

On Saturday, the eight amateur chefs competed in the Great Garlic Cook-Off. The winner was Suzanne Clark, from Phoenix, Arizona, with a sarsaparilla glazed Wild West burger and southwest sweet potatoes. It was Suzanne's first visit to the Garlic Capital.

On Sunday, garlic Showdown champion, Jason Gronlund, became emotional when he was crowned champion for the third year in a row. Gronlund is the Vice President of Culinary for Smokey Bones Bar & Fire Grill in Orlando, Florida. He donated his $5,000 prize winnings back to the Garlic Festival in honor of two gentlemen who had died since last year's competition: Jay Minzer, who had been his sous-chef the year before, and Peter Ciccarelli, who had handled media relations for the Garlic Festival since 1997. The popular host of the Food Network program "The Chew," Carla Hall, hosted the competition.

When it was all over, President Mercado noted, "In addition to the money that's distributed to non-profit groups every year, the Festival has also contributed to a number of improvements that benefit residents all year long, including the gorgeous new amphitheater, additional trees and the new Mulberry Picnic Area at Christmas Hill Park."

Years after his presidency, Vito Mercado recalls a situation that exemplifies "the whatever it takes spirit of the volunteers." It was Saturday evening at about 8:30 pm when he ran into Tom Cline, the incoming President, coming back into the park. It appeared that one area of the park grounds had not been cleared of debris. Vito turned around and, along with Cline and a small group of volunteers, cleaned the area in the dark so that it was ready for the Sunday morning visitors. 🧄

Attendance
80,848

What Was New
$300K Given to Non-Profits
$10,673,000 to Non-Profits Since 1979

Installation of Wi-Fi System

First Three Day Pass for Locals

Volunteer of the Year
Ron Perez (Utilities)

Queen Brittany Souza

Gilroy **Garlic Festival**
July 25, 26, & 27, 2014

Art Poster by Aliza Alkoby, Tarzana

DOLLARS RAISED FOR LOCAL CHARITIES SINCE 1979:
$10,366,251
THE GILROY GARLIC FESTIVAL THANKS YOU!

Ryan and Nikki Dequinn

INTERESTING TIDBIT —

Keeping it All in the Family

The brother and sister duo of Ryan and Nikki Dequinn started volunteering at the Festival for their respective sports teams while in high school. In 2014, Ryan was the chairman of the tickets committee and Nikki was the assistant chairwoman of the advisory committee. To the Dequinns, volunteering is second nature.

"I think the fact that we're getting so many people together—all the kids (softball, baseball, basketball, water polo)— is amazing. It benefits our kids, the coaches, and the many different groups involved. To see it all come together is awesome," noted Ryan.

kids workshop

Karaoke

face painting

It's All About The Kids!

fun rides

bubble fun

Herbie

Ronald McDonald

family fun

Elvis & Mr. Garli

Fun at the Garlic Festival

entertainment & queens

Many of the four million visitors to the Gilroy Garlic Festival since 1979 have been youngsters or teenagers. To accommodate this growing population of Festival goers, the Festival added a children's area sometime in the early '80s. Over the years the **Children's Area** has grown substantially in size and offerings. Today it is a major operation with multiple locations. Chair, Becky Whiteside and Char Marazzo, Assistant Chair, oversee this multifaceted operation.

In the Children's Area, just south of Gourmet Alley, there are a host of activities for younger kids. There is everything from quiet play areas to somewhat wild rides, bounce houses, entertainment, crafts, food, vendor booths and face painting. The place is crazy noisy with screams,

laughter, and fun. While no one keeps count of how many people enter the Children's Area, Chair Whiteside notes that nearly all of the thousand popsicles, hot dogs, and water-melon cups were gone by Sunday evening.

The Children's Stage is hosted by Lori & RJ of Cotton Candy Express. There

is continuous entertainment from 11:30 am to well after 5 pm each day. Lori Moitié has been on the Children's Stage for years. Lori & RJ have a high-energy style that makes everything fun and upbeat. Actually, Lori and a former group, Rainbow 65, worked the Amphitheater Stage. Entertainment on the Children's

INSET: Children's Area Assistant Chair, Char Marrazzo and Chair, Becky Whiteside

Stage covers the gamut from song to clowns, magic, puppets, groups, violins, folklorico, Ronald McDonald and celebrity visits from the Garlic Festival Queen and her court…all coordinated by Lori& RJ.

Way over in the southeast corner is the Teen Zone. This area has a variety of attractions and food for the older kids…a zip line, rope maze, mechanical bull, fun slide, a mash house, air brushing,

temporary tattoos and, of course, food.

Between the two areas, over by the Cook-Off Stage is safe, secure and immensely entertaining rock climbing wall.

How does all this happen? Whiteside and Marazzo use about 120 volunteers from Christopher High School Cheer, Relay for Live: Perez Fighters, the Boy Scouts and Adams 4H. There are also donations of produce from B&T Farms

and support for Ronald McDonald for the local McDonalds, care of Steve and Jan Peat. One of the more "noisy" contributors is Home Depot with their construction projects. Kids, with parent's help, nail and glue any one of a number of free wooden toys. The Home Depot leader, Tim Beckley, and his Home Depot helpers distributed 4,000 donated kits! A special shout out

to Home Depot! The Santa Cruz Beach Boardwalk and Wriggling Brothers Circus also provided tickets for prizes and discount coupons.

We have all heard that it takes a village to raise a child. For three days a year the Garlic Festival builds a village to help with that task!

The Board of Directors

David Reynolds
Vice-President

Gwyneth Sauceda
Secretary

Brent Jenkins
Treasurer

Deanna Franklin
President

Vito Mercado
Past President

Nikki Dequin
Director

Ric Heinzen
Director

Kurt Svardal
Director

Mike Zukowski
Director

From cleaning tables at age eight to becoming the President of the 37th Garlic Festival, **Deanna Franklin** said the ultimate food fair represents tradition, an incredible volunteer team, a love of Gilroy—and something she calls "Garlic Festival magic."

"We talk about Festival magic all the time in the (Garlic Festival) Association. Festival magic is when something is not going as planned, but it turns out better than planned," said Franklin, a Gilroy native. "Every time someone drops the ball, ten people are ready to step in. That's Garlic Festival magic."

Franklin started volunteering in volunteer hospitality. "Our job was to clean tables. I was chopping onions. I was doing whatever at that age. I sold programs for field hockey in high school," Franklin said.

Franklin had helped out on the Cook-Off Stage for about seven years, serving as the assistant chair and the chair. She then served on the Garlic Festival Board for three years. She first stepped up to be the secretary of the Garlic Festival before becoming the vice president in 2014.

"I'm not done. I'm far from being done," Franklin said. "I'm seeing what I will do next. I still want to volunteer. I can't give it up. It's in my blood."

She has passed down that love of volunteering to her two sons. Over the years, they have helped get the Cook-Off Stage ready, hung signs, and worked in the Children's Area.

"I just really enjoy giving back to the community, and through the Festival, you're impacting so many non-profit organizations and schools," Franklin said. "When I'm there, I know that every second and every minute that I put into the Festival, someone in the community is benefiting. That's huge for me. It's that warm feeling of giving back to the community that I was raised in, and I raise my kids in."

Franklin said she is happy to give her time to a Festival that is the envy of so many cities and has given more than $10 million to local non-profit groups.

"When you think about 4,000 volunteers coming together and giving their blood, sweat, and tears for a three-day event, that's incredible," she said.

Franklin said new additions to the 2015 Garlic Festival include a Garlic Dream Wedding contest. One couple will be selected to get married or renew their vows in a garlic-themed ceremony on the Cook-Off Stage during the Festival on July 26.

The Gourmet Alley Demonstration Stage will also be larger this year to allow more interaction with the guests. Festival attendees will have the chance to sample new recipes that may become a new dish in Gourmet Alley, Franklin said.

"We really want the attendees to feel a part of it in the coming years. If we don't have their input, what will be their motivation to come back?" Franklin said. "That's how the Festival is so successful. The board comes up with new ideas. Then they reach out to the chairs to get their input."

"The ultimate goal is for everyone to come together and have fun and know that you're giving back to your community," she said.

Attendance
95,095

What Was New

$250K Given to Non-Profits

Garlic Dream Wedding Contest

Enlarged Demonstration Stage

Volunteer of the Year

Erin Monroe (Recipe Contest)

Queen Bridget Brown

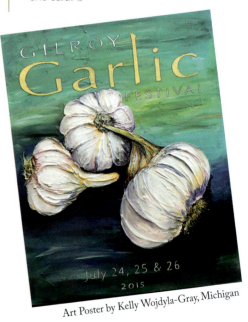

Art Poster by Kelly Wojdyla-Gray, Michigan

A Legacy of Memories...

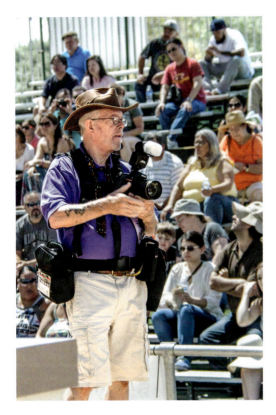

Compliments of Bill Strange

In 1982, Bill Strange went to the 4th annual Gilroy Garlic Festival with his camera in hand. Using his keen eye, he snapped some photos, developed them, and gave them to Dick Nicholls, the Festival's executive director at the time, expecting nothing more than a thank you. Instead, he got a job offer.

Nicholls asked Strange to be the Festival's official photographer, an offer he eagerly accepted for a post he has held ever since.

"It's like a big family reunion every year," Strange said. "(I love) being part of something that's successful and that's done so much for the community."

Strange moved to Gilroy in 1979, which also happened to be the year of the very first Garlic Festival. He recalls its quaint beginnings at the junction of Highway 101 and State Route 25 before moving to its current location at Christmas Hill Park. At that time, the Festival was limited to just Christmas Hill Park, and Strange recalls attendees being shoulder to shoulder, all wanting to revel in the garlicky goodness.

Strange has seen the Festival change and expand into a culinary destination. But through its transformation, one thing has stayed the same: the dedication of the Festival's volunteers.

"I love the spirit of all the volunteers, of what everybody does," Strange said. "It's a real camaraderie with all the volunteers and all the people that work just so well together. They inspire you to do this for the community."

For more than three decades, he has hustled from one side of the park to the other, shooting everything he can all three days from open to close. And the money Strange has raised volunteering goes directly to Rebekah Children's Services.

"I can't even put into words how generous he is with his time and his expertise," said Gilroy Garlic Festival Assistant Executive Director Joann Kessler, alongside Strange since 1990.

Strange's photos are used year-round by the Gilroy Garlic Festival Association for its website and promotional materials, among other things. He also photographed the association's advisory committee and committee chairs in addition to pre-Festival events such as the Garlic Queen competition.

It's been a long, engaging, and garlic-filled road for Strange, and he has a plethora of treasured photos to remember it by. His most memorable moment was when he literally helped save a life.

He and former Dispatch photographer Lora Schraft happened upon a service dog suffering from heatstroke, and they immediately radioed for help. That was the year that Dennis Harrigan, a veterinarian, was President. He set up an IV for the dog, which saved its life.

"I felt pretty good about that. Dennis told me if it had been any longer, the dog would've never made it," Strange said.

Such memories have become even more valuable to Strange as he's no longer living in Gilroy. Though he moved two hours northeast to Oakdale, he notes that the Festival's people keep him coming back. Plus, Kessler jokes that she won't let him retire.

"I told him that he can't retire until I retire—and don't ask me when I'm going to retire," she said with a laugh. "I think it keeps him young."

Strange agrees, and said attendees can expect to see him at Festivals for many more years to come.

"People say, 'you gonna do it next year?' and I say, 'I don't know.' I'm getting older," Strange said. "But as long as I'm physically able, I will keep coming back each year."

Bill Strange retired in 2016.

Special Thanks

To the official
Gilroy Garlic Festival
Association photographers
Bill Strange and Lora Schraft
for capturing the essence of
the 37th Annual Gilroy
Garlic Festival 2015.

Alexis Higgins
and SakaBozzo

The Start of Something Scrumptious

Anyone who has been around the Gilroy Garlic Festival for the last 37 years knows to expect a surprise or two. There is always something to wake the senses… the sights…the sounds…the smells…the people…the weather.

The 2015 Garlic Festival had plenty of "wake-ups." The weather was perfect, the crowds manageable and the "feel" up beat and positive. One of those events took place on the Cook Off Stage Friday afternoon. Local celebrity chefs **Gene Sakahara** and **Sam Bozzo**, the SakaBozzo twins, "separated at birth," appeared again. This duo has been mixing comedic banter and cooking for twenty-one years. For years the two, one Italian and one Japanese, have combined a rapid-fire fun-loving dialogue with some great cooking tips

and techniques. But on Friday they might have met their match in a 10-year old St. Mary's student.

Alexis Higgins was a contestant on Fox's Master Chef Junior this last January 2015. Alexis, one of the youngest contestants, did well but was eliminated from the show, but not from cooking appearances. This unique young lady has a remarkable confidence and some pretty significant cooking skills. After a recent tour of Pulmuone Foods (producers of Monterey Gourmet Foods) here in Gilroy she was asked to compete with the in-house chef and to prepare a meal. In deference to her age the planners set out a small chef's knife on her workstation. She immediately asked for a "real knife" and proceeded to prepare a delicious entre using some of the

Monterey Gourmet Foods products. The consensus in the kitchen that night was that it was too close to call a winner.

On stage at the Garlic Festival Alexis joined SakaBozzo in preparing three dishes: Alexis, Garlic Mushrooms, Sam Bozzo, Kale and Italian Sausage, Gene Sakahara, Penne alla Boscaiola. Alexis got assistance from Sam and Gene but also helped the two prepare their dishes. In addition to the food, three things stood out …this kid knows how to cook, she has fun doing it and she can banter with the best of them. SakaBozzo might have more years together on stage than Alexis has age but she stood there strong and confident. SakaBozzo got a real-life, up-close-and-personal taste of the future.

Local Restaurant Owners Participate in Iron Chef Style Competition

The Garlic Showdown is a Sunday event at the Garlic Festival. The event is an Iron Chef style competition. Four professional chefs compete for a grand prize of $5,000.

The Garlic Festival attracts visitors form all over the world. The Saturday Great Cook-Off attracts amateur competitors from all over the United States. California Universities compete for the Friday Garlic Bowl and on Sunday, professional chefs from the Bay Area compete in the Garlic Showdown. This year one of the chefs was Gilroy restaurant owner, **Adam Sanchez**, and his restaurant partner and sous chef for the day, **Ann Zyburra**. Adam and Ann are owners of the Milias Restaurant in downtown Gilroy. The other competitors were Jonathan Toste of Willard Hicks restaurant in Campbell; Danae McLaughlin of the Harker Schools in San Jose; and Chad Greer of LB Steak in San Jose.

Shortly before the competition the competitors were introduced to a some-what limited pantry and the mystery ingredients: baby cucumbers, Spam, Dole fruit cocktail, and squash blossoms. Competitors had to prepare two dishes, one chicken and one pork loin. The competition was timed. In less than two hours, dishes were prepared, served and judged.

While Adam and Ann did not win, they admitted to having fun and were pleased with their final dishes. The mystery ingredients were a challenge… most fine dining establishments do not use a lot of Spam or fruit cocktail. The penny sized baby cucumbers were an unknown entity. The squash blossoms fit in nicely. Congratulations to our local celebrity chefs!

The judges agreed the final entrees were delicious all around and the final scores were very close. The 2015 winner was Jonathan Toste from Willard Hicks. Daphne Oz, co-host of ABC's The Chew and three-time Showdown winner Chef Jason Gronlund, hosted the event. Chef Gronlund is currently the Vice-President of Culinary for the Orlando based Smokey Bones Bar & Grill. Chef Gronlund donated his 2014 prize money to the Gilroy Foundation.

What would you make with baby cucumbers, Spam, Dole fruit cocktail and squash blossoms?

The Board of Directors

Mike Zukowski
Vice-President

Todd Trekell
Secretary

Jim Buessing
Treasurer

David Reynolds
President

Deanna Franklin
Past President

Randy Wong
Director

Rick Heinzen
Director

Lisa Sheedy
Director

Doug Stewart
Director

The 2016 Festival was an opportunity for President **Dave Reynolds** to use his financial skills to move the Festival to a more sustainable future.

Over the years, the Festival became a renowned food Festival. However, the finances of the Festival were less solid. In the early years, the Festival grew and prospered. In the later years, obligations outgrew income. Dave was able to use his financial knowledge to start the journey to a more solid financial standing. Dave has a background in finance, managing securities trading on the Central Coast for JP Morgan Chase. Dave is currently the CEO of Trevis Berry Transportation. Dave set out to address the financial issues while bolstering the spirit of volunteers and upping the community awareness of the benefits of the Festival.

Dave reduced expenses and increased revenue while giving over $284,000 to volunteers' non-profits. "Lots of people stepped up – typical Gilroy," he noted. The Festival contributed to Christmas Hill Park improvements to the tune of $170,000.

"My skillset in running businesses and organizations fits perfectly with running the garlic Festival," Reynolds says. "We've looked at these challenges, of busing expenses that have exploded and just running an entirely volunteer-run organization as efficiently as possible to save money everywhere we can."

"We will continue to strive for the highest quality food, the best entertainment," said Reynolds. "We're excited about the way the Festival came together, the work that everybody put in. Now we're just focusing on continuing to make it better and better every year.

The volunteers are basically the secret sauce of the Festival. We do it just for the love of garlic, the love of Gilroy, and the growth of community."

Being a numbers guy he offers these "by the numbers":

• On average, attendees gobble down 2 tons of fresh garlic from Christopher Ranch per Festival.

• The Festival Association, which plans the shindig every year, has given out close to $11 million to local non-profits since its founding in 1979

• More than 4,000 volunteers work to put on the Festival, representing 140 non-profit groups in Gilroy and nearby areas.

• Since 1979, more than 4 million people have flocked to the Festival. 🧄

Art Poster by Sherri Harig, Arizona

Attendance
95,095

What Was New
$284K Given to Non-Profits
Champions of Charity Cook-Off
Battle of Backyard Amateur BBQers
Paid Parking

Volunteer of the Year
Deanna Parker (Parking)

Queen Kyle Perez-Robinson

Chamber of Commerce Beer Concession

From the very first Gilroy Garlic Festival, ice-cold beer enhanced the social atmosphere that brought visitors together to enjoy food, art, and music. To keep up with the demand for the popular beverage, the Gilroy Chamber of Commerce kept the taps flowing. By the mid-80s, over 1,800 kegs of beer were served, a remarkable feat and one that would bring valuable dollars into the coffers.

As a result of this important fundraiser, The Chamber became an anomaly throughout the Chamber industry with its independence from City funding, purchasing its facility in downtown Gilroy, and initiating model programs to stimulate economic and leadership development.

Through strategic planning and the spirit of collaboration, The Chamber initiated the Gilroy Visitors Bureau, the Gilroy Economic Development Corporation, Leadership Gilroy, Gilroy Political Action Committee, and many other partnerships to ensure economic vitality. The Chamber also became the go-to Garlic Festival resource for alcohol management training for every organization serving alcohol at the event.

Gilroy has become a tourist destination, a retail hub, an industrial magnet, and a community with a 'Spice for Life.' So, with every mug of beer that was raised in a toast to that proverbial spice, we affectionately call garlic, the Chamber thanks the millions of guests who 'sipped the suds' and made our community great. Cheers!!

2016 Loses

Joann Kessler retired from her position as Assistant Executive Director after 26 years of service.

Chris Filice, Office Manager, was let go due to budget cuts, after 21 years of service.

Festival Cooking Comic Show, **SakaBozzo** —Twins Separated at Birth retired (25 Years).

Robert James Dyer (real estate developer, long time Festival supporter (38 Years) passed away.

Mr. Garlic, **Gerry Foisy,** who donned the famous garlic bulb for 29 years, retired and passed the suit on to his son.

News From the Cook-Off Stage — 2016 Winners

Cal Fire Capt. Herb Alpers and his last minute partner retired firefighter Tom Evans won the $3,000 prize for the Muscular Dystrophy Association"

Amateur chef Rebecka Evans from Danville, CA claimed the 2016 Great Garlic Cook-Off crown – and a $5,000 cash prize –with her original recipe, "Garlic Goat Cheese Bacon Soufflé with Creamy Garlic Mustard Sauce".

Owner and Executive Chef Michael Fisher from Fisher's Delicatessen & Catering in Hollister won the annual Garlic Showdown.

At the first-ever battle of backyard BBQers at the Gilroy Garlic Festival, SHOWOFF BBQ from Salinas, CA emerged the winner in the Garli-Que Backyard BBQ Rib Throwdown competition.

Queen Kyle at first flame up of the day, and with Chanel Lucid (8 years old) who had been designated as the pageant's junior princess. She plans to be a contestant in 2026 when she's eligible.

Three Days in the Life of a Festival Queen

We met up with the Queen Kyle Perez-Robinson and her court at 8 am at the Princess Palace—the name of the motorhome provided by Jeanine Koloski, Assistant Chair Children's Area.

From 8 to 9 am, the girls prepped for their day; making sure every hair was in place and sashes in order. Queen Pageant Chair, Lauren Mantani (who looks like she could be one of the girls — only the lack of a crown and red Festival shirt set her apart) went over the schedule to let the girls know what to expect. The mood was light and cheery with last-minute curling iron exchanges, selfies and small talk. One of the girls practiced her speech for the dinner they were to attend that evening. To the casual observer, they would appear to be a group of best friends who had known each other for many years.

As we strolled over to their first assignment, the lighting of the garlic bulb, I had the opportunity to discuss the Festival with Queen Kyle. "I'm really excited, I've

never really seen the Festival from this side; I'm usually a volunteer, either helping my mother in her booth at the Arts & Crafts area or working in Gourmet Alley for the high school choir. It will be fun to see it from a different angle," she said.

Kyle's best friend (since second grade) Brittini Bombino is one of her princesses. Neither girl had told the other of her plan to apply for the Garlic Festival scholarship pageant. This fall, Brittini is attending the prestigious AMDA (American Musical Drama Academy) in Hollywood, CA, and Kyle will be attending Stanford University in Palo Alto. It was through SKYPE that the subject came up and they found out that they had both applied. Once they realized they would be taking this journey together, the pageant and all its trimmings seemed just a little less of a challenge, and more of a bonding adventure.

While "having it all" is something most of us only lust after, Kyle, at the young age of 23, just does. She's bright, attractive, talented and self-disciplined. At Stanford,

she is majoring in Human Biology (concentration in the biological and social determinants of maternal and infant health) and has applied for a Co-Term Masters program in Community Health & Prevention Research. Kyle spent the summer working in a research lab studying language acquisition in low-income Spanish-speaking communities, the result of which is a program that teaches mothers alternative ways of talking to kids to improve the quality of their speech. Data and research will help Latino parents in "how to influence their children to succeed when in school." She is also working on a series of children's books in Spanish—to help parents communicate with their smaller children. The lab was run by Anne Fernald.

The 40-hour weekly commitment made it a little "difficult" because some of her pre-Festival duties required long commutes during rush hour traffic. But she enjoyed them all.

In addition to her studies at Stanford, Kyle is very active in the arts. She is on the

For the Festival Queen and her court, the morning started with a stop at Starbucks for coffee and Nob Hill/Raley's for supplies in their official Festival van. Once at the Festival, they prepped for their day before heading over to the lighting of the torch and the opening day activities.

executive board of Ram's Head Theatrical Society serving as the theatrical resources manager for props and costumes and as an assistant costume designer for their spring show, "Rent." She was also an actress in two other productions during the past twelve months. During her time at Stanford, she's sung in the choir (although not this last year) and has sung the national anthem at various Stanford sporting events.

Kyle would like to take some time off between going for her PhD or MD program to travel and live abroad for a year.

Queen Kyle Perez-Robinson with her court: Alrene Garnica, Brittini Bombino, Jasmine Cruz, Julia Chizanskos, Angelique Lucero, Amber Harding, Marille Gomez with Queen Pageant Chair Lauren Mantani and Assistant Chair, Katie Alatorre.

The Board of Directors

Todd Trekell
Vice-President

Randy Wong
Secretary

Jim Buessing
Treasurer

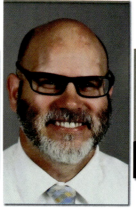

Mike Zukowski
President

Dave Reynolds
Past President

Shawn Keck
Director

Cindy Fellows
Director

George Minerva
Director

John Zekanoski
Director

Bigger, Better and Bolder was the motto of the Festival organizers for the 2017 event. And they did not disappoint. Each volunteer committee was driven to develop tangible solutions for a better customer experience. Everything lined-up perfectly. And the Festival goers were "in the mood" to enjoy a fantastic line-up of celebrity guests and great music. "The flow was perfect," according to President **Mike Zukowski**. As a result, attendance and revenue were up.

Zukowski is a local therapist and Gilroy resident. His journey to the President's position came through one of the more challenging Festival assignments, parking. Mike attributes the success of the Festival to the volunteers and committee chairs who "have the ability to deal with the unexpected." A good example of this was a problem with the port-a-potties. The 2017 Festival had a new vendor. Somehow the new vendor did not get the message that the bathroom units needed to be cleaned and emptied as soon as the Festival closed on Friday evening. After numerous calls and much anxiety,

the units were cleaned and ready to go Saturday morning, even while the gates were opening!

Mike and the 2017 Board implemented several changes to the Festival. Food Network celebrity chefs Giada De Laurentiis and Shaun O'Neale hosted cooking competitions on the cook-of stage. De Laurentiis starred in her own Food Network show "Giada at Home." O'Neale was the winner of the seventh season of the Food Network show, Masterchef. The Food Network filmed a special edition of Giada's Garlic show for a later time slot.

Another example was the Rotary Wine Pavilion which moved from the sunny Ranch side of the Festival to the former children's area and became the Rotary Wine Garden. The move was a big success for all. The children's area moved west of the amphitheater and was expanded.

The amphitheater became a country western stage with sponsorship from KRTY and hosted a dynamite list of entertainers, including the up-and-coming Carly Pierce.

A new dish deep fried, Gilroy Garlic Shrimp, was introduced in Gourmet Alley.

The Garlic Train railed down from San Jose on Saturday and Sunday.

The 2017 Festival did not have a program but it did have a great little pocket map and a computer app with up-to-date info on the Festival.

Outside of the Festival there was a boost from McDonalds who hosted a national advertising campaign for a

limited special Gilroy Garlic Fries.

On the cookoff stage Friday Shaun O'Neale hosted the Champions for Charity event won by EMT John Campbell and paramedic Morgan Sanders of AMR Santa Clara County.

On Friday representatives from The Guinness Book of World Records presented official recognition for the "largest attendance at a garlic Festival." The record was set in 2011 with a certified attendance record of 109,067.

On Saturday Shaun also hosted the

Attendance
102,667

What Was New
Wine Pavilion Moved to Park Side
Children's Area Moved By Amphitheater
Induction into Guinness World Records

Volunteers of the Year
Lindsey Buessing (Queen Pageant)

Queen Maggie Pickford

Art Poster by Diane Grosman, Florida

LEFT: Gilroy's own Carlos Pineda, Rebekah Children's Services' Culinary Academy and Kneaded Bakery wins Garlic Showdown.

BELOW: Gilroy Rotary Club spearheaded the "Be The Match" campaign locally. Over 5,000 people have registered since 2000.

Garlic Festival Makes the GUINNESS WORLD RECORDS

Plaque (l):In a special ceremony on Friday, representatives from GUINNESS WORLD RECORDS ® officially certified the Festival as the world record holder for largest attendance at a garlic Festival.

The record was set July 29-31, 2011, with a total audited attendance of 109,067.

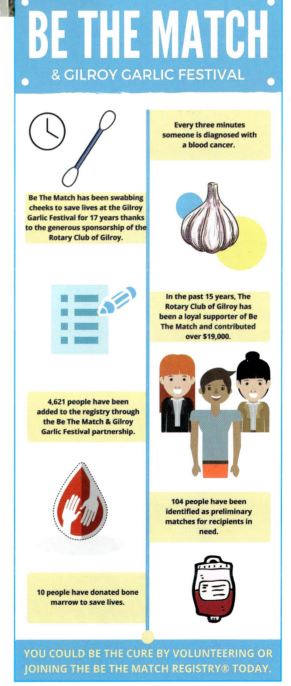

BE THE MATCH
& GILROY GARLIC FESTIVAL

Every three minutes someone is diagnosed with a blood cancer.

Be The Match has been swabbing cheeks to save lives at the Gilroy Garlic Festival for 17 years thanks to the generous sponsorship of the Rotary Club of Gilroy.

In the past 15 years, The Rotary Club of Gilroy has been a loyal supporter of Be The Match and contributed over $19,000.

4,621 people have been added to the registry through the Be The Match & Gilroy Garlic Festival partnership.

104 people have been identified as preliminary matches for recipients in need.

10 people have donated bone marrow to save lives.

Garlic Cook Off which was won by Naylet LaRochelle, of Miami, Florida with her original recipe for "Smoky Salsa Roja Shrimp and Roasted Garlic Cotija Grits."

On Sunday Giada De Laurentiis and the Food Network hosted the Garlic

Showdown where four professional chefs competed in an "Iron Chef" style of competition. Local Carlos Pineda of Rebekah Children's Services' Culinary Academy and Kneaded Bakery won. 🧄

"Everything came together…it was a whirl wind. People had incredible energy. Among the volunteers there is a remarkable camaraderie…this thing is huge..it is a national, even international event—but it is built on a great tradition."

President Mike Zukowski

YOU COULD BE THE CURE BY VOLUNTEERING OR JOINING THE BE THE MATCH REGISTRY® TODAY.

ROTARY CLUB OF GILROY
NEW WINE GARDEN

The 2017 Gilroy Garlic Festival promised to be a Bigger, Better, Bolder Gilroy Garlic Festival…and in many ways it was! Giada De Laurentiis was a hit on the Cook-Off Stage. Local chef, Carlos Pineda from Rebekah Children's Services, won the Iron Chef-style "Garlic Showdown." The Festival garnered an entry in the Guinness World Records as the world's largest garlic festival with the 2011 Festival having an attendance of 109,067. The 2017 Festival almost hit the 103 thousand mark, not a new record but an improvement from 2016. The 2017 Festival also had some big name music, an official Kansas City BBQ contest, a new children's area and a new wine area.

The new Rotary Wine Garden had some Rotarians worried that this major fundraiser would be too radical a departure from the tried and true Rotary Wine Tent. From all indicators the new bigger, better, bolder Wine Garden was a hit. Gross revenues were up over 35 percent. While final bills have yet to be paid and net revenues have still to be calculated, the revenues from this Rotary Fundraiser look good. The proceeds will go into the Rotary Endowment which benefits local Rotary projects, scholarships and grants.

Another great indicator was that there were fewer cases of wine left over, several wineries ran out of wine and some wineries that had not participated in the past said they would be in next year. Winemakers and owners who visited the Garden commented favorably on the layout, the crowds, and the buzz. One even noted that it felt like being at a big winery party. Some wineries, during the Garlic Festival Weekend, noticed customers at the winery with fliers from the Rotary Wine Garden.

Operation Share Life was also successful at the new location. They signed up 250 potential donors with 45 percent of those being minorities who are underrepresented in the bone marrow registry. Operation Share Life is part of the international "Be the Match" program which is a global leader in bone marrow transplantation conducting research to improve transplant outcomes, provide support and resources for patients, and partner with a global network.

The Rotary Wine Garden also had a positive impact in an unexpected area. For mixed couples, that is where one drinks wine and the other beer, the Wine Garden allowed them to stay together and enjoy the shade, misters, wine and beer. Another positive was the continuing flow of people through the Wine Garden. In the old Wine Pavilion, there was only one entrance and visitors sometimes camped out in the cool of the tent. In the 2017 Wine Garden, there seemed to be plenty of interaction and movement of people in and out of the area. Most movement was accompanied by a big smile and "Salute" or "Salud" or "Cheers" or "Campai" or "Prost" or "Cin Cin" or "Saude" or "Proost" or "A votre sante" or "Sláinte" or simply "Enjoy."

Much credit goes to Rod Pintello, the Rotary Wine Garden chairperson and his daughter, Whitney Pintello, the 2017-18 Rotary President…and Rotarians, winery staff and friends who staffed the over 350 volunteer Wine Garden slots.

"Change is the law of life. And those who look only to the past or present are certain to miss the future."

John F. Kennedy

In 2017, the local **Gilroy Sister Cities Association** hosted five of Gilroy's six Sister Cities. Representatives from Takko-Machi, Japan (Sister City connection 1988), Angra do Heroismo, Portugal (Sister City connection 2004), Tecate, Mexico, Saint-Clar, France (Sister City connection 1985), and Koror, Republic of Palau (Sister City connection 1994) toured Gilroy and attended the Gilroy Garlic Festival.
The only city not able to attend was Monticelli d' Ongina, Italy (Sister City connection 1985).
The Gilroy Sister Cities Association was established to take advantage of the unique opportunities that Sister Cities programs offer in improving international relations at an individual, personal level.

Garlic Festival Programs

For the first 38 years of the Garlic Festival printed programs were available for Festival goers. In 2017 the Garlic Festival Association produced an official map brochure. Eventually as digital technology became more available, the Festival Association produced a fully digital program available for viewing on smart phones.

For the first few years the Garlic Festival Association prepared a simple program or brochure for each Festival. Eventually the Association worked with The Gilroy Dispatch staff to produce the annual program. The photo above represents 21 of those programs. These programs are from the private collection of Barbara Trekell who worked on program sales at the Garlic Festival from 1992 to 2016.

In addition to the official Garlic Festival Program the Dispatch often produced a Festival Guide in its regular newspaper. The local Miracle Miles, a free advertising magazine, also produced a Festival Guide for many years.

Gilroy Garlic Festival: Top 10 Can't-Miss

1. Watch the **Pyro Chef Flame-Ups** on Gourmet Alley

2. Catch a cooking competition on the **Garlic Cook-Off Stage**

3. Browse the **Arts & Crafts** galleries on both sides of the park

4. Try the world-famous garlicky food on **Gourmet Alley**

5. Dance with friends at the **Amphitheater Stage**

6. Sample local wines in the new **Wine Garden**

7. Shop for official Festival souvenirs at the **Garlic Mercantile stores**

8. Check out the fun **Children's Area**

9. Snap a selfie in front of the **Burning Bulb**

10. Try the **FREE Garlic Ice Cream!**

RANC

GATE 5

Yellow Lot
Pink Lot

Garlic Avenue

Blue Lo
Green Lo

MILLER A

ATM	Administration	Arts and Crafts	BBQ Challenge
Beer Garden	Bike Parking	Burning Bulb	CalTrain Shuttle
Children's Area	Fire Services	First Aid	Food Vendors
Free Garlic Ice Cream	Garlic Braiding	Garlic Cook-Off Stage	Garlic Fries
Garlic Grove	Garlic Mercantile	Gazebo Stage	Gourmet Alley
Media Tent	Police	Pyro Chef Flame-Ups	Rain Tent
Restrooms	Rock Climbing Walls	Security CheckPoint	Shade Tents
Shuttle Bus	Vineyard Stage	Volunteer Check-in	Volunteer Hub & Pub
Wine Garden	Zip Line		

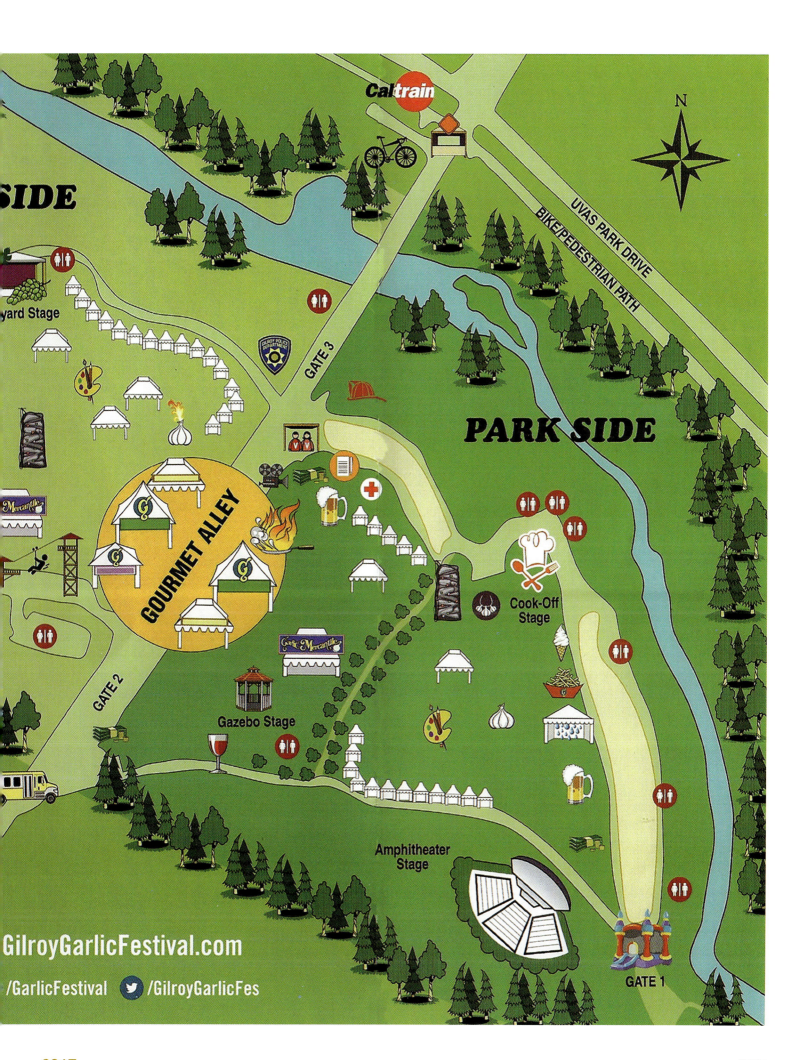

Caltrain

UVAS PARK DRIVE

BIKE/PEDESTRIAN PATH

N

SIDE

yard Stage

Mercantile

GATE 3

GATE 2

GOURMET ALLEY

PARK SIDE

Garlic Mercantile

Gazebo Stage

Cook-Off Stage

Amphitheater Stage

GATE 1

GilroyGarlicFestival.com

/GarlicFestival /GilroyGarlicFes

2017

Shaun O'Neale hosted the Champions for Charity event won by EMT John Campbell and paramedic Morgan Sanders of AMR Santa Clara County. Sakabozzo judged the event.

The Board of Directors

Shawn Keck
Vice-President

Virginia Alegre
Secretary

Tom Cline
Treasurer

Todd Trekell
President

Mike Zukowski
Past President

Lauren Mantani
Director

Ariele Combs
Director

Jennifer Speno
Director

John Zekanoski
Director

The 2018 President **Todd Trekell** grew up with the Festival. He attended his first Festival in 1993, helping his teacher mom sell lemonade. He moved on to sell programs, help out in Gourmet Alley, and eventually become a co-chair in the Alley before getting elected to the Board and assuming the President's position in 2018.

Todd gives credit where it is due.

"As board president, a very important part of my job is making sure the spotlight stays on all those volunteers who are still in the trenches doing all the hard work to keep raising money for our local schools, charities, and non-profit groups. They are the true heroes. They are the reason the Festival has continued to succeed all these years. Everyone who's ever worked at the Festival should take great pride in the $11.7 million we've raised for these worthy organizations."

The 2018 Festival ran smoothly in spite of some challenges with a new parking arrangement. The Garlic Train again brought visitors from the north on Saturday and Sunday. The Garlic Festival App, introduced in 2017, proved itself very successful and valuable. Online ticket sales continued to grow. Christopher Ranch sponsored prepackaged bulbs of garlic to the first 4,000 visitors each day. Finally, the Festival introduced the Festival Mule, a signature drink in a copper mug.

On the music side of the Festival, The 40th Annual Gilroy Garlic Festival had a great line-up. The bands made up a great mix of blues, rock, country, soul, funk, southern rock, surf rock, rockabilly, dance music, party bands, and a DJ tent with a wide variety of local DJs. Some of the acts in 2018 were: The Moondance Band, The Tsunami Band, Angelique Lucero, Ted Sanchez, The Mike Osborn Band, Tin Man, Vital Sign, blues singer Paula Harris, Los High Tops with singer Chantilly Lace Vincent and a Santa Cruz favorite, Extra Large.

This year, for the first time, the Festival had the Garlic Clove Dance Tent presented by 99.7 NOW! with live local DJs spinning tracks all weekend long.

Art Poster by Chris Dufur, Gilroy

President Todd Trekell summed the year up at the annual dinner in January 2019:

"To me, the Gilroy Garlic Festival is a mindset, it is a conversation starter, it is a spot on the map, it is a rite of passage, a shared experience amongst old friends and new, it is the glue that keeps this City of 58,000 residents feeling more like a town of 20,000 and most importantly, it is a family."

Todd Trekell, 2018 President

Attendance
80,646

What Was New
$255K Given to Non-Profits

Garlic Chef Jr. Competition

Volunteer of the Year
Rob Graham (H$_2$O Crew)

Queen Sloane Pace

PLAQUE HONORING FOUNDERS INSTALLED
at Christmas Hill Park

Garlic Festival Founders

Don Christopher, Val Filice & Rudy Melone spearheaded the formation of the Gilroy Garlic Festival. The first Festival was held in 1979. Annually, over 4000 volunteers work the Festival to provide financial benefits to charities and non-profit groups while promoting the community of Gilroy through the celebration of garlic. The Garlic Festival has returned millions of dollars to the community. The first Gourmet Alley, in this park setting, was held here in the Mulberry Picnic area.
Dedicated July 2018

Donors: Karen & Don Christopher, Bob Filice, Gloria Melone & Family, Janice & Tim Filice, Gilroy Foundation, Headstart Nursery, Gilroy Garlic Festival, Barbara & Ed Mauro, Gilroy Chamber of Commerce, SakaBozzo, Kathryn & Gene Sakahara, Judy & Sam Bozzo, Gavilan College Education Foundation, RaboBank, Camille McCormack

With special thanks to: Karen Aitken, Bill Strange, Greg Bozzo, Mark Zappa
In Collaboration with: The City of Gilroy & The City of Gilroy Public Art Committee

Honorees and descendents in photo:
Founder, Don Christopher and son, Bill; Valerie and Bob Filice (Founder Val Filice's children); and Gloria Melone (Founder Rudy Melone's wife).

On Thursday July 26, 2018, the evening before the opening of the 40th Gilroy Garlic Festival, there was a unique gathering at Christmas Hill Park. Many past and present Garlic Festival presidents, board members and guests gathered to dedicate a plaque honoring the founders of the Festival. In attendance were members of Rudy Melone's and Val Filice's families and Don Christopher along with members of his family.

LEFT:
The Champions for Charity cooking challenge, was won by John Campbell and Morgan Sanders from AMR Santa Clara County. For the second year in a row, they donated their winnings to the Alzheimer's Association.

RIGHT:
For the second year in a row, Chef Carlos Pineda from the Culinary Academy and Kneaded Bakery at Rebekah's Children's Services in Gilroy won the "Garlic Show-down" competition. The $3,000 prize was given directly to the Rebekah's Children's Services Culinary Academy.

Will Simbol from New York, NY claimed the Great Garlic Cook-Off award of $5,000 for his Savory Crunchy Freshy Tangy Shrimpy Herby Garlic Lumpia Wrap.

The new "Herbie" mascot was a huge hit!

The **Gilroy Garlic Festival Association** announced distributions totaling $255,000 to 170 different charities and non-profit organizations. The 2018 figure brings the Garlic Festival's 40-year total distributions to over $11.7 million.

On September 20, 2018, the Gilroy Unified School District recognized the… Gilroy Garlic Festival and presented the Board of Directors with a plaque thanking Festival organizers for their "tireless commitment, philanthropic vision, community leadership and unwavering support" of Gilroy schools.

Todd Trekell, President of the 2018 Gilroy Garlic Festival, "We are proud to partner with students and staff from Gilroy schools every year to help raise money for schools in our community. The enthusiasm and energy of our volunteers are a huge reason for the Gilroy Garlic Festival's lasting success."

In the brand-new Garlic Chef Jr. competition, hosted by O'Neale on Friday afternoon, eight young chefs faced off for the chance to win a notebook computer valued at $500. The top prize winner was Addyson Dell, age 6, who needed a stool to reach the stove but still wowed the judges with her Garlic Mac N Cheese with Crispy Garlic Chicken Tenders and Roasted Asparagus. *(See pages 230-231.)*

CENTER (l-r): Second Runner-Up Searra Harding, **Queen Sloane Pace**, First Runner-Up Maricel Gomez. **PRINCESSES** (l-r): Jennesa Andrade, Kylie Kuwada, Sophia Blocher, Melinda Colbert, Frida Arias, Adrianna Molina, and Lauryn Longoria.

First Garlic Chef Jr. Competition

Eight Young Amateur Chefs Competed for the Top Honors

Addyson Dell, age 6, won with her Garlic Mac N Cheeese with Crispy Garlic chicken.

The Board of Directors

Tom Cline
Vice-President

Virginia Alegre
Secretary

Jeff Speno
Treasurer

Shawn Keck
President

Todd Trekell
Past President

Jim Buessing
Director

Lauren Mantani
Director

Ed Struzik
Director

Kurt Svardal
Director

To the world, the 2019 Gilroy Garlic Festival will be remembered as the site of yet another mass shooting. But in the world of Festivals, it will be recognized as the 41st successful Garlic Festival. And the one that got its finances back on track.

The 2019 Gilroy Garlic Festival President, **Shawn Keck**, an event producer by trade and a long-time Garlic Festival volunteer, is proud to have had a leadership role in the Festival. He notes that attendance for the 2019 Gilroy Garlic Festival was up more than five percent, at 84,830. Gross income for 2019 was projected to be about 13 percent higher, at $3.08M. Expenses remained flat at $3.13M, and the net loss was only $100,000. The previous year ran a much higher deficit. In 2019 The Festival gave $250,000 to 155 local charities and non-profit organizations, which brings the Gilroy Garlic Festival's 41-year total distributions to over $12 million.

The Festival also built upon the success of last year's signature cocktail, the Mule, with a new one this year—the Whiskey Daisy, a whiskey sour made with Jameson.

Foodies were excited that things were mixed thing up a little at Gourmet Alley as well. "Traditionally, there has only been one window for each food item, but in 2019, guests were able to purchase multiple items at one window. They could order a sandwich, fries, and garlic bread at once and pick it all up at once in a streamlined food experience, which helped reduce Gourmet Alley lines.

"We wanted to make it a little easier for folks to get the great food we had available to them," Keck said.

Other highlights included: bundled tickets (admission, a combo plate from Gourmet Alley, and parking) were available at South Bay Area Costco stores—at significant savings, and the red and light blue Gilroy Garlic Festival logo was branded as "the" logo of the Garlic Festival!

On Friday, Champions for Charity was won by Bret Baker and Gayle Gaggero, US Army. They gave the prize money to the Gary Sinise Foundation. The US Army team competed on behalf of the Gilroy Veterans' Hall.

Also, on Friday, eight aspiring young chefs competed in the Garlic Chef Jr. Competition. Local Kaiden Gonzales (age 12) won with his Crab Cakes and Good Fortune Spring Rolls.

On Saturday, Gary Exner from Wilsonville, Oregon, who made a Strawberry Tart with Garlic Shiso Cream and Yuzu Glaze, won the amateur Great Garlic Cook-Off. Top Chef head judge Tom Colicchio, who later did a cooking demonstration, hosted the event. Also, on Saturday, Real Housewives of New Jersey star and cookbook author Teresa Giudice prepared some of her family's favorite Italian dishes.

On the other side of the park, professional BBQ teams did battle in the Garli-Que BBQ Challenge.

Local Chef Carlos Pineda won his third Garlic Showdown for his Mixed Herb and Red Beet Pan-Seared Quail and Rib Eye Steak. Chef Carlos donated his 2019 prize winnings to the Gilroy Foundation.

Attendance
84,830

What Was New

Bundled Tickets

Signature Drink; Whiskey Daisy

Saturday Concert:
Colbie Caillat (Gone West)

Queen Kylie Kuwada

Art Poster by Chloe Crossman, California

The backbone of the Festival…
Our Volunteers!

"Together, we basically get to build Disneyland in a week —then tear it down. It's an amazing event to be part of. Everyone is working for the same reasons: to raise money for the community and throw a party for nearly 100,000 people."

Shawn Keck
President

At a press conference Sunday evening, Brian Bowe, Executive Director of the Gilroy Garlic Festival, told reporters: "Gilroy is an amazing, tightly-knit community. We are family. We have had the wonderful opportunity in this community to celebrate our family through our Garlic Festival, and for over four decades that Festival has been our annual family reunion. It's such a sad, just horribly upsetting circumstance that this happened on the third and final day of this year's Festival."

Shawn Keck, President of the 2019 Gilroy Garlic Festival, spoke in support of the more than 4,000 volunteers who worked to organize and host the annual Festival: "We are heartbroken that senseless violence brought this year's Festival to such a terrible and tragic end. We are truly grateful to the Gilroy Police Department, who responded immediately to prevent further loss of life, and to the hundreds of other first responders from regional and federal agencies who have provided additional support. We are also thankful for the thoughts and prayers and outpouring of support from people all over the world."

On Sunday, July 28, 2019,

On Sunday, July 28, 2019, the Garlic Festival, the City of Gilroy, the families of victims, and all of Gilroy experienced an unbelievable horror. We will probably never understand the anger that led a young man to think that hurting people would justify the hurt he felt. Aside from a few who misguidedly directed anger at this young man, the community came together in a truly remarkable way. It was downright extraordinary. According to Donna Pray of the Gilroy Foundation, it shows a level of community caring, compassion, and involvement that is "inspiring. "

We heard stories of individuals, families, groups, organizations, and businesses who stepped up and helped every day. Volumes could be written about them. We highlight a few of the many examples here. We refrained from including names because this is about the community, not the individuals. Our goal is not to heap praise but to celebrate a community that is #GILROYSTRONG.

When the tragic incident began, many people ran away from what they thought was the source of the shooting—as they rightfully should—while others ran towards the scene to help. Some were local police officers who helped bring the tragic violence to a quick ending. Others were regular citizens who cared for the injured, transported folks to the hospital and helped others evacuate. Nurses immediately notified local hospital facilities to be on alert while other medical personnel and first responders did their job, ignoring the danger. Contracted bus drivers and school bus drivers safely evacuated hundreds of Festival attendees. Local officials, bystanders, and first responders moved people to safe areas like the amphitheater and established a perimeter for fear of a second shooter.

Others courageously comforted panicked adults, children, vendors, and families. And still, others transported or took in strangers in the surrounding neighborhoods while waiting for an all-clear. These collective and individual acts made a difference.

By 7:45 PM that night, two hours after the shooting, the Silicon Valley Community Foundation was in touch with the Gilroy Foundation to set up a victims' fund. By 1:37 PM the next day, the Gilroy Foundation received its first PayPal donation of $25. Since that time, the Gilroy Garlic Festival Victims Relief Fund has received over $1.9 million. Donations have come in all shapes and sizes. The largest was an anonymous $250,000 donation; the smallest was $5 with a note that it was all they could afford!

Less than 24 hours after the event, ordinary citizens organized a vigil where kids set up a lemonade stand and raised over $3,600. A national chain restaurant pledged a percentage of sales to generate over $11,000. A real estate office gathered donations from friends, relatives, and clients to generate over $57,000. T-shirt shops donated stock and labor to generate a variety of #GilroyStrong t-shirts, hats, and bumper stickers. A group of young teens used their own money to purchase beads and supplies to produce GilroyStong bracelets. Another real estate office set up letters to the families of Stephen, Kyla, and Trevor—three young people who tragically died from gunshot wounds. People made badges, hats, and wristbands. Folks organized vigils and memorials. Restaurants and wineries hosted benefits. A local artist distributed 500 #GilroyStrong painted rocks around Gilroy. Bay Area professional sports teams hosted events and collected donations. The band performing near the shooting scene set up a donation station at their next concert. A traveling out-of-state band waived their fees to host an evening benefit at a local music venue. A bookkeeper's daughter offered to do a spreadsheet categorizing the donations to the Gilroy Foundation. One restaurant owner returned to his kitchen Sunday night and made 50 pizzas for the first responders. One local spent a few hundred dollars on energy bars and snacks for the first responders. The local rodeo paid tribute to #GilroyStrong. A local Zumba class delivered a box with $344 in cash. Martial arts dojos collected funds. A local restaurant hosted a regional hockey team's fundraiser.

Garlic Festival Association personnel and volunteers worked with law enforcement to identify vendors, volunteers, and guests who needed to retrieve valuables and vehicles. Area police departments offered extended support and assistance. Local social service agencies stepped up to provide counseling and support. The school district provided first responder gathering locations and counseling for returning students. The local community college offered space for recovery and reunification.

The Gilroy Foundation worked with the Ventura Community Foundation, which had previously experienced a similar tragedy, to set up applications and procedures for distributing the Gilroy Garlic Festival Victims Fund. The distribution of funds was overseen by a committee of Gilroy Foundation and Silicon Valley Community Foundation volunteers. Allocation of funds began on August 15 and concluded on December 31, 2019.

These vignettes represent only a fraction of the good, courageous, remarkable, kind, compassionate, and generous things people have done in response to this tragedy. The preponderance of love demonstrated and delivered to Gilroy far outweighs the hate that sparked the tragedy. The good displayed cannot overcome the life-taking or the physical and emotional pain many have suffered, but it can be a beacon of hope. There are thousands more untold stories of courage, dedication, caring, and assistance.

The fact is that Gilroy came together in a way that surpasses the expected resources of this community. All of this means that we have a strong Gilroy, and it is bigger and much more capable than this tragic event. We are a capable and caring community…

(Originally published in gmhTODAY, 2019)

THANK YOU GILROY PD

#GILROYSTRONG

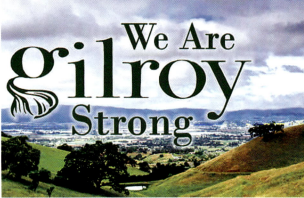

We Are gilroy Strong

CAR WASH

GILROYSTRONG

Gilroy STRONG

Garlic City

We Stand as one

#408

GILROY FUERTE

GILROY is home!

Gilroy Strong

"When I was a boy and I would see scary things in the news, my mother would say to me 'Look for the HELPERS. You will always find people who are helping.'"
— Mr. Fred Rodgers

Buttons $5

The Board of Directors (2020-2021)

Jeff Speno
Vice-President

Cindy Fellows
Secretary

Trevor Van Laar
Treasurer

Tom Kline
President

Shawn Keck
Past President

Jim Buessing
Director (2020)

Brad Royston
Director

Greg Bozzo
Director

Mike Wanzong
Director

Janet Krulee
Director (2020)

March 20, 2020
Gilroy Garlic Festival Association

Announcement From the Gilroy Garlic Festival

"For over four decades, the community has been at the heart of the Gilroy Garlic Festival. Our volunteers, vendors, sponsors and guests have generously supported our more than 150 local charities.

Given the unprecedented national emergency we face and its unknown trajectory, we must put the health and well-being of our community first. Sadly, this means we are unable to host the Festival this year.

We are postponing the Gilroy Garlic Festival to July 23-25, 2021. The Gilroy Garlic Festival Association looks forward to welcoming you in 2021 for the best Festival ever."

Lawn signs were placed throughout Gilroy announcing the coming of a revised version of the Festival in 2021.

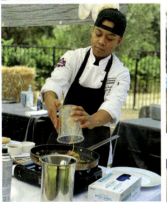

2020 Garlic cLOVE Days

The unique thing about the 2020 Garlic Festival was that it was not! The aftermath of the 2019 shooting and the Covid pandemic set the conditions for not holding a Festival. However, this did not slow a determined group of Gilroy Strong individuals. Every year since 1998, there has been a Leadership Gilroy program. One essential component of the yearlong community leadership program is a community project which hones and tests the participant's leadership skills. In 2020 the Leadership Class initiated a unique, multi-faceted project: Garlic cLOVE Days.

First off, there was a Clove Challenge, somewhat like the Ice Bucket Challenge. Video yourself eating a clove of raw garlic, challenge three others to do the same, or make a pledge to a local non-profit and post the video. This component brought in over $8,000.

Secondly, the class set up tables at local stores to sell cLOVE merchandise in person and/or purchase merchandise on the web.

Thirdly, on what would have been the three days of the Festival, classmates divided up and held virtual and in-person events.

Friday, July 24th, was cLOVE Community Awareness Day focused on local non-profits and small businesses that hosted live streaming, interviews and cooking demonstrations.

Saturday, July 25th, was a "get active" day with in-person and virtual events. Gilroy Gardens hosted four events limited to 50 people at an approved social distance for yoga, conditioning, fitness, and biking/running. Gilroy residents were encouraged to exercise individually or in family groups safely.

Finally, on Sunday, July 26th, there was a flurry of virtual and in-person activity with safe distancing celebrations called cLOVE the Block, a citywide street-by-street, driveway-by-driveway block party. Neighbors were encouraged to organize their own fun safely in their driveways, focusing on food, family, friends, and fun while celebrating Gilroy's resiliency. At 5:30 pm, there was a 30-second moment of unity and reflection followed by the ringing of the cLOVE Day bells. Hearing the bells clanging around town was heartwarming.

The Leadership Class of 2020 raised over $40,000, which was distributed to seven non-profits: Rebekah Children's Services, Operation Freedom Paws, Unravel Pediatric Cancer, Live Oak Adult Day Care, Community Solutions, Gilroy Compassion Center, and St. Joseph Family Center.

The Gilroy Leadership Class of 2020 was recognized for its efforts by receiving the 2021 Community Service Award from Gavilan College. The Gilroy Chamber of Commerce awarded Leadership Gilroy with the 2021 Educator of the Year Award with special recognition to the Garlic cLOVE Days project.

"In a time when there was a huge void due to the cancellation of the Gilroy Garlic Festival and the COVID pandemic, they brought something meaningful to Gilroy and the people that love this town!"

Gavilan College

Year Forty-Two **2021**

In 2021, the Gilroy Garlic Festival Was Reimagined.

"It's been interesting, to say the least. I'm honored to have maintained my spot, and the continuity of the Festival."

"Everyone has a real desire to see the Festival return, and that's where our focus lies."

Tom Cline, 2021 President

Limited Gourmet Alley

Drive-Thru Only Gourmet Alley (July 23-25 & July 30-August 1)

For two weekends in July, Gilroy Presbyterian Church hosted a drive through pick-up of juicy pepper steak and sausage sandwiches, succulent scampi, garlic fries and garlic bread. While drivers waited for their orders, the volunteers performed the famous Gourmet Alley flame-ups and the controlled dance of volunteers prepping the take home delights.

Farm to Table Dinner

Farm to Table Dinner (July 24)

This elegant four course dinner was held at Fortino Winery. Each dish was prepared by Executive Chef, Diane Sturla from Relish Kitchen & Drink and paired with an exceptional Fortino wine. The ingredients for the dinner were sourced from local farmers and purveyors, in keeping with the Festival's commitment to local agriculture.

Sponsors of the dinner included several local businesses contributing back to the community: Chiala Farms, Christopher Ranch, Cline Glass, Frantoio Grove, GB Landscape Services, GN USA Sales, Inc, Headstart Nursery, Mission Valley Ford Trucks, and Pinnacle Bank.

It was a great evening with a great mix of Garlic Festival supporters, past presidents, former board members and good people. The evening included a series of video tributes to the Festival and the victims of the 2019 shooting.

Gilroy Garlic Festival Golf Classic

Garlic Festival Golf Tournament (July 30)
A host of golfers gathered at the Gilroy Golf Course for the 2021 tournament and dinner. The event was a bit of a throwback to the first Festival golf tournament held in 1979.

2022

The Gilroy Garlic Festival is Not Over

Greg Bozzo wrote this column on behalf of the Gilroy Garlic Festival Association Board of Directors, Jeff Speno, Trevor Van Laar, Cindy Fellows, Mike Wanzong, Brad Royston, Paul Nadeau and Tom Cline. It appeared in the Gilroy Dispatch on May 4, 2022.

On April 21, the Gilroy Garlic Festival Association (GGFA) released a statement that the Garlic Festival was postponed indefinitely due to prohibitive insurance required by the City of Gilroy.

We stand by that statement. Some of the talk online against the city and council is speculative, incorrect, divisive and should stop. We agree with the mayor, when she says, the City of Gilroy is all of us. Some news reports and discussions around town have been incorrect: The Garlic Festival has not closed forever. Even as a 2022 event has been canceled, we are looking for possibilities in 2023.

Make no mistake, the tragedy of 2019 is precisely why we are in this predicament. The board of directors has made public the challenges associated with busing and housing developments. However, decades of GGFA volunteers have worked hard to preserve finances to be positioned well in challenging times. Our association does not wish to be subsidized by the City of Gilroy.

The GGFA has worked hard to reduce expenses to benefit local charities. This can't be done without the help of donors, landowners and agencies such as Gilroy Unified School District and Gavilan College. At the 2019 Festival, our association, GUSD, a private bus company and local farmers formed a plan and cut over $100,000 in expenses from previous years.

When chaos erupted on the evening of July 28, 2019, it was Gilroy bus drivers who turned back and drove toward a very tense situation to help evacuate guests. In addition, GUSD has allowed use of its kitchens for decades. Anyone who suggests that GUSD does not participate in the success of the Garlic Festival is wrong.

The pandemic canceled a 2020 event. By fall of the same year we signed an agreement with the Gilroy Gardens administration to hold a 2021 event in their lower grounds. That agreement was then halted by the Gilroy Gardens Board. Gilroy Gardens never put a price tag on holding an event there. Their only requirement was to meet City of Gilroy insurance requirements. Since then, the Gilroy Gardens administration and board have stopped all negotiations with the GGFA.

When we found ourselves without a site, we turned to Gavilan College. At Gavilan we found a culture of transparency and a willingness to help from staff, administration and the Board of Trustees. Insurance costs were not prohibitive at all. The GGFA decided against Gavilan because the land offered could not meet our needs.

The GGFA has been committed to the citizens and especially to the City of Gilroy for over 40 years. The $12 million-plus in contributions does not include money raised by others. The Chamber of Commerce, Gilroy Foundation, Rotary, Gavilan Football, El Roble, etc., have raised millions more. Years ago, there was an economic impact report on the benefits of the Garlic Festival. When considering shopping, gas, hotels, restaurants, sales tax, etc., the impact was $6 million!

GGFA has also made sure many of its givings would be so everyone could benefit. Below are some.

Christmas Hill Park:

• 1990s: $400,000 to City of Gilroy to speed up the development of the west side of the park.

• 2009: $42,000 for synthetic grass near the playground.

• 2011: $225,000 in co-sponsor matching funds with Christopher Ranch/Family to rebuild Amphitheater

• 2014: $225,000 to rebuild Mulberry Picnic area.

• 2018: $150,000 for asphalt road to Solorsano School area.

GUSD:

• 2007: $200,000 contribution for Gilroy High Cafeteria.

Our association respects the challenges of operating a city. While some there believe the costs connected to finding a creative solution to a Festival rebirth are too high, we believe that the costs not to do so are even higher.

Special Recognitions

Putting this book together was a challenge. We reviewed over 3,000 pages of newspaper articles, as well as a multitude of Festival brochures, programs, annual reports and various other materials. We also looked at over 150,000 slides, photos and digital images. Much of the material we used in this book came from two main sources:

The Gilroy Dispatch (archived at the Gilroy Museum and in The Dispatch's digital archives)
The Gilroy Garlic Festival Association

The **Gilroy Garlic Festival** began in 1979 as a community celebration of garlic. It went on to become an internationally known Festival that attracted over 4.4 million visitors. The Festival generated over 800,000 volunteer hours. Over $12 million was donated back to local non-profits. During its peak, it was estimated that the Festival generated between $6-8 million annually in local economic impact.

Back when it started there were no long-term plans. Things matured and evolved. Only after the first Festival did the founders institute the payback to non-profits based on the number of hours donated by volunteers. The Festival did not have a paid employees till its third Festival in 1981. During the 42 years documented in this book, it only ever had a maximum of three paid employees. The original logo used in 1979 persists to this day, with only an annual color change.

The **Gilroy Dispatch** traces its lineage to the Gilroy Advocate, which first published on September 12, 1868. In 1925, The Dispatch opened as competition to the Advocate. In 1930 the two merged to form the Gilroy Evening Dispatch. The Dispatch went through a variety of changes from 1930 to 2014 including owners in Australia and New Zealand. It has gone from a six day a week publication to a once-a-week publication.

In 2014 Silicon Valley-based Metro Newspapers, headed by Dan Pulcrano purchased The Dispatch, along with three other weeklies. This marked the first time in 36 years that The Dispatch returned to regional ownership.

The Dispatch, a weekly publication, is currently head-quartered in downtown Gilroy at 7455 Monterey Road. The Hollister Free Lance and the Morgan Hill Times are sister newspapers.

The Gilroy Museum, at Fifth Street, has archived copies of The Advocate and The Dispatch from 1868 to the current day.

Contributors

They say it takes a "village to raise a child." In writing this book we have come to realize that it took a larger-than-average village to put this book together. We hope we have recognized everyone who contributed to the book, but odds are we may have missed someone and for that we apologize.

Dave Bouchard, Executive Director 1981-86

Sam Bozzo, GGFA President 1990

Jan Bernstein Chargin

Don & Karen Christopher

Tom Cline, GGFA President 2020-21

Pat DeStasio

Susan Dodd

Edith Edde

Tim Filice, GGFA President 1982

Chris Filice, GGFA Former Office Manager

Valerie Filice

gmhTODAY Magazine

Gilroy Dispatch

Gilroy Garlic Festival Past Presidents

Gilroy Life

Gilroy Museum: Susan Voss & Joe Robinson

Norie Goforth

Andrea Habing

Jim Habing, GGFA President 2000

Linda Hussar

Kathy Katavich

Joanne Kessler, GGFA Former Assistant Director

Karen LaCorte

Ed Mauro, GGFA President 1997

Frank Mendiola, Musician (Garlic Songs)

Paul Nadeau, GGFA Board Member 2022

Brigitte Nicholls

Carol Peters

Connie Rogers

SJ Mercury News

Jeff Speno, GGFA President 2022

Barbara Trekell

Ted Uchida

Susan Valenta

Photographers

Special recognition is due to the Garlic Festival photographers. The Festival Association and many local photographers gave us access to over 150,000 photographs, slides and digital images. The following list acknowledges the photographers that we were able to identify:

Bill Strange—Official Festival Photographer (1982-2016)

R & S Baker

Karl Bonfert

Randy Dotta-Dovidio

Teri Freedman

Lee Gasser

Tommy Gibson

Huck Hagenbuch

Carrol Hurd

Joe Marus

Jim McDonald

Ana Mercalo

James Mohs

Christopher Murphy

Laura Schraft

John A. White, Jr.

This book is dedicated to the Gilroy Garlic Festival's founding fathers:
Don Christopher, Val Filice and Rudy Melone.

And to the star of the event…GARLIC!